A PUGET SOUND ORCA IN CAPTIVITY

A PUGET SOUND ORCA IN CAPTIVITY

The Fight to Bring Lolita Home

SANDRA POLLARD

Foreword by David Neiwert,
author of *Of Orcas and Men: What Killer Whales Can Teach Us*

THE
History
PRESS

Published by The History Press
Charleston, SC
www.historypress.com

First published 2019

Manufactured in the United States

ISBN 9781467140379

Library of Congress Control Number: 2018958989

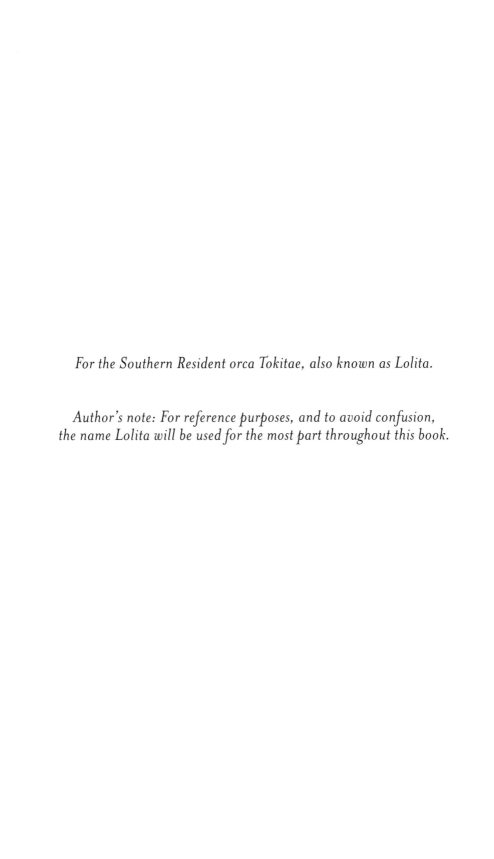

For the Southern Resident orca Tokitae, also known as Lolita.

Author's note: For reference purposes, and to avoid confusion, the name Lolita will be used for the most part throughout this book.

CONTENTS

FOREWORD

I f you go up to the railing of the orca tank at Miami Seaquarium before the show, sometimes Lolita will come over to say hello. She likes to look people in the eye when she does. And it can be unnerving.

The eye of a fifty-year-old killer whale is a deep pool unto itself, and it always reveals a mind and a presence that is more than merely intelligent but possesses a depth beyond our ability to understand. Looking into Lolita's eye, one sees the strength of will that has enabled her to sustain herself all these years.

This is even more remarkable when you look at the tank where she has lived for over forty-five years now. It's hard to convey in words, or even with photos or videos, how shockingly small the crumbling old concrete tank where she lives really is. It's actually mind-boggling that she could have survived so long in a space so tiny.

The last time I visited the Seaquarium to see Lolita—no, I'm sorry, I mean Tokitae, her real name; the one her owners have called her for four decades is an atrocity—the audience was mainly composed of tourists fresh off the boat from South America. A man from Colombia was next to me as Tokitae came over and said hello. We chatted.

He wanted to know how long she had been in that tank. I told him. Was she captured from the wild? She was, I said—from a population of orcas I know intimately. And this tank, he asked—is this just for shows? Do they have a bigger tank where she spends her time off?

No, I said, smiling wryly. If only that were the case. This is the tank where she has been for over forty years. Every minute of them.

He shook his head.

If only he knew the full story.

Sandra Pollard has now given us the ability to tell Tokitae's whole story, by pulling together all the known facts in the case and rendering a complete picture of how she came to be in captivity, how she survived and how her defenders back in her home waters in the Salish Sea have mounted a tireless campaign to return her and retire her in those waters.

One look in her eye should be enough to convince anyone that it is the least we can do to honor a spirit so stout and a heart so big.

—David Neiwert

PREFACE

ollowing the publication of *Puget Sound Whales for Sale: The Fight to End Orca Hunting* in 2014, I had no immediate plans to write another book. The story of the iconic Southern Residents' fight for survival—and their continuing battle to avoid extinction—had been told. By 1987, all the known Southern Residents brutally ripped from their families in Washington State and British Columbia, Canada, between 1964 and 1973 and sold to marine parks around the world had died.

All, that is, but one. Her name is Tokitae, also known as Lolita. She is the only surviving Southern Resident from that tragic era following her capture on August 8, 1970, in Penn Cove on Whidbey Island, Washington State, one of the most notorious capture events depicted in detail in *Puget Sound Whales for Sale*.

Although I touched on her sad story, I knew there was much more to be said. Against all the odds, she has survived in a tiny, barren tank at the Miami Seaquarium, Florida, with no other orca for company since the loss of her companion, Hugo, in 1980. While her surviving family now swim wild and free, she is expected to earn her keep by performing twice daily for a public hungry for entertainment.

For over twenty years, Susan Berta and Howard Garrett, co-founders of the nonprofit whale sightings and education organization Orca Network, formed in 2001, have campaigned to bring Lolita home to her natal waters. The more I learned about their dedicated attempts to raise awareness of Lolita's situation, the more I realized that this was a

Dr. Ingrid N. Visser (*left*) and the author on San Juan Island, July 2015. *Richard Snowberger*.

story that needed to be told. When I mentioned to orca researcher Dr. Ingrid N. Visser after Superpod 2015 (an annual gathering of authors, filmmakers, researchers and "orca dorks" held on San Juan Island, Washington State) that I wasn't sure whether I could do Lolita's story justice, she replied, "But you have to do it—you have to do it for Lolita." Fortunately, thanks to Garrett's industrious record-keeping and regular Lolita updates throughout the campaign, the thread was in place to weave the story together.

The aim of this book is to endeavor to convey Lolita's strength and fortitude and the sheer magnitude of the efforts of Garrett, Berta and other determined, compassionate individuals to rescue Lolita from her enforced confinement and an attempt to portray the struggles and complexities involved in the prolonged fight to return her to her family. There have been numerous hurdles to overcome, involving petitions, lawsuits, bureaucratic lassitude and obfuscation, agency maladministration, corporate greed and the misconceptions of an often misguided and misinformed public. The convoluted path to justice for Lolita has taken many twists and turns, encompassing disappointments and triumphs along the way.

The book is a tribute to Lolita's stoicism and ability to survive, isolated from her kin while forced to share an unnatural, cramped environment with Pacific white-sided dolphins (known as "lags," a term derived from their scientific name, *Lagenorhynchus obliquidens*) that perpetually harass her.

Everyone likes a story to have a happy ending. As this book goes to print, the last chapter, titled "Hope for the Future," remains just that in the hope that, one day soon, Lolita will come home.

ACKNOWLEDGEMENTS

Once again. I am indebted to Susan Berta and Howard Garrett for their help and assistance throughout the research and writing process.

I wish to express my gratitude to Dr. Ingrid N. Visser, Orca Research Trust, New Zealand, for her encouragement, professional expertise and generous provision of images; to marine mammal biologist Dr. Terrell Newby for permission to use images of the 1970 Penn Cove capture at which he was present; to longtime orca advocate and former secretary of state Ralph Munro (1980–2001), for his unwavering support of the campaign to bring Lolita home.

Thank you, also, to the many other contributors, including Ric O'Barry (Dolphin Project), David Ellifrit (Center for Whale Research), Carrie Sapp, Sandy Dubpernell, Deanna Carpenter and my mother, Doreen Semmens, who had the unforgettable experience of meeting the capricious orca Luna in 2004.

Garrett's half brother Kenneth C. Balcomb III, principal researcher at the Center for Whale Research, San Juan Island, Washington State, prepared and presented the meticulously contrived plan for Lolita's return/rehabilitation/release more than twenty years ago. He has remained true to the original concept and steadfastly maintained faith in the proposal in the face of opposition.

Often the voices of children are the most powerful. The kids who formed Lolita's Legion and sent hundreds of letters and colorful drawings in support of Lolita's release to senators and other officials over the years deserve special recognition. More recently, in the digital age, Chloe Shapiro, a fifth grader at Nova Southeastern University in Davie, Florida, started *Kids for Whales* and created both a PowerPoint presentation for fourth graders and a play to raise awareness about whales in captivity. Her mother, Diana Shapiro, grew up in Miami and was taken to see Lolita when she was a child. She remembers the sadness she felt and that same raw emotion reflected in Lolita's eyes.

As always, thank you to my husband, Richard Snowberger, who has supported and encouraged in every way possible the completion of this book. His technical skills have been invaluable in ensuring that all images were up to the required standard for publication. Some of those images would not have been possible if it were not for Cindy and Monte Hughes of Mystic Sea Charters, Anacortes, who have provided the opportunity to spend time on the water, where I have enjoyed the privilege of encountering Lolita's extended family and observing the many facets of their natural behavior in the wild.

My appreciation, too, for commissioning editor Laurie Krill's patience and support and The History Press's professional teamwork. Thank you, also, to copyeditor Audrey Mackaman for all her help.

My greatest hope is that the hopes and dreams of all who seek retirement for Lolita will be realized and that she will know once again the freedom so despicably stolen from her all those years ago.

*Places of confinement providing free food and medical care
are called prisons.*

—Dr. John C. Lilly

1

STOLEN FREEDOM

They did not let her go..."

Those were the words of television station KING 5 News commentator Don McGaffin when he witnessed the August 1971 Penn Cove orca capture. McGaffin and cameraman Jeff Mart risked life and limb to obtain graphic footage of the harrowing event in which fifteen to twenty-four whales were captured by infamous orca hunters Edward "Ted" Griffin and Donald Goldsberry, who had plied their dubious trade since 1965. The three whales selected on this occasion for distribution to marine parks were from the now endangered Southern Resident community, comprising three pods, J, K and L, that frequent the waters of Washington State and British Columbia—a fourth whale was freeze-branded and released back to the wild.

The whale to which McGaffin referred was probably Kona, a fourteen-foot female calf about six years old and a member of L pod. McGaffin watched as she was belted to the side of a purse seiner, the start of her journey to SeaWorld, San Diego, California, where, for the rest of her short life, she would perform tricks for the public.

Those same words could have been used to describe a similar event that took place almost a year to the day earlier in August 1970, when Griffin and Goldsberry drove the Southern Residents, then totaling over one hundred whales, into Penn Cove. Seven of those whales were destined for delivery to marine parks around the world. There was no law at that time to regulate the hunting and capture of killer whales.

Map of the Salish Sea. *Courtesy Stefan Freelan, Western Washington University.*

Don McGaffin and cameraman, 1971 Penn Cove capture. *Game Department Photographic Collection, Washington State Archives.*

The last of the whales torn from her family in the 1970 Penn Cove roundup was Lolita, also a member of L pod. She, like Kona, was a calf around four to six years of age, but unlike Kona, who died in 1977, Lolita is still alive and performing for the public at her original destination, the Miami Seaquarium, Florida.

Many other notable events made headlines that year: the launch of the failed Apollo 13 space mission, the first 747 commercial flight from John F. Kennedy Airport to London Heathrow, celebration of the first Earth Day on April 22, the breakup of the Beatles and the deaths of rock stars Jimi Hendrix and Janis Joplin. But nothing intruded quite so deeply into the minds of Whidbey Island residents as the state and nationwide news coverage of the notorious Penn Cove capture. Susan Konopik, a Whidbey Island resident, recalls how as a child she and her friends cried in frustration at the sight of the trapped whales. In her memoir of those tragic events, she wrote, "It was wrong, it was horrible, and we knew we were too small to do anything about it." Konopik feels a deep sense of sorrow at the memory. She and her friends still talk about those childhood images. "We always wonder about Lolita. We really didn't know their names. Seems like something that beautiful just shouldn't have a name to it."

Many years later, Carey Tremaine, one of the divers hired to assist the capture team, who was paid $75 a day during the most intense stage of the capture, described how the calves cried as they were forcibly separated from their mothers. Despite their fear, the mothers' deep maternal instincts dictated the action they needed to take to save their precious offspring. Tremaine witnessed a female nuzzle against her calf and attempt to force off the tight noose encircling the calf in a vise-like grip. He described it as "an act of beauty, bravery, intelligence and athletic ability."

The mother's efforts to rescue her calf failed. While she watched, the child she had nurtured from the womb was lashed to the side of the capture pen. Trapped and alone, the calf watched and waited as the netting at one end of the pen was opened to release the larger adults. While the rest of the distressed whales circled and milled nearby, trying in vain to gather their fractured family together, the calf's mother kept vigil near the capture pen, repeatedly spy-hopping in a desperate attempt to maintain contact with her offspring, calling and calling in the pod's unique dialect—all the time, the helpless calf, in confusion and fear, cried to be reunited with her mother, a sound Tremaine and others will never forget. That calf was probably Lolita, a member of the Southern Resident L25 sub-pod (a grouping of matrilines that spend more than 95 percent of their time together). She, like her presumed mother, Ocean Sun (L25), has displayed the same attributes of beauty, bravery, intelligence and athletic ability while enduring almost half a century of enslavement, mostly alone.

As McGaffin reported on camera from Penn Cove in 1971, "If you could hear those sorrowful tones and those grieving cries tearing at you, perhaps you could hear distant voices pleading…let her go…let her go."

Spotter planes, speeding boats and a barrage of exploding seal bombs to disorient, deafen and petrify were the cruel reality of life for many killer whales in Washington State and British Columbia between 1965 and 1976. Harpoon guns, tranquilizer darts and purse-seining nets were the methods

Trussed in a net, injured and bleeding (possibly Lolita), 1970 Penn Cove capture. *Terrell C. Newby, PhD.*

No escape. 1970 Penn Cove capture. *Terrell C. Newby, Ph.D.*

implemented by Griffin and Goldsberry, the principal perpetrators of the lucrative trade in orca hunting, to capture these iconic creatures.

Most of the whales targeted were young, as they were easier to train and transport, resulting in the significant loss of a breeding generation from which the Southern Resident population has yet to recover. In addition to those whales "collected" for commercial purposes, at least thirteen more drowned or died from injuries sustained as a result of the violence inflicted during the capture operations.

Following the whales' seizure and before selection and delivery to their designated marine parks, Griffin and Goldsberry transported them to the Seattle Marine Aquarium at Pier 56, Alaskan Way, Seattle, where Griffin had operated since June 1962. As with all the captives, after divers manhandled and maneuvered Lolita into a canvas sling, she was hoisted from the water by crane and lowered onto a mattress on a waiting flatbed truck parked on the old Standard Oil dock at San de Fuca overlooking Penn Cove. Her journey from here would be on either the Clinton/Mukilteo ferry, which connects the south end of Whidbey Island with the mainland, or by road crossing the Deception Pass Bridge to the north, which joins Whidbey to Fidalgo Island and subsequently the mainland.

Captured orca on the Clinton/Mukilteo ferry, August 10, 1970. *Deanna Carpenter.*

Penn Cove capture, 1971. *Game Department Photographic Collection, Washington State Archives.*

On arrival at the Seattle Marine Aquarium, the procedure was reversed. After being hoisted by crane from the flatbed truck, Lolita was lowered into a concrete-sided tank to join the rest of the captured whales.

Orcas in the wild know no boundaries. During the winter months, the fish-eating Southern Resident orcas range between southeast Alaska and Monterey, California, in pursuit of their favored food, high-energy Chinook salmon, which constitutes 80 percent of their diet. In the fall, the orcas make forays into Puget Sound in search of winter Chinook and their second choice of salmon, chum, while in the spring and summer months they spend much of their time in the inland waters of the Salish Sea, an area comprising the Strait of Georgia, the Strait of Juan de Fuca and Puget Sound. Because some whales had drowned at the Seattle Marine Aquarium due to disorientation, they were "walked" around the perimeter of the saltwater tank by aquarium employees to familiarize them with their surroundings. Drugs and antibiotics were administered to offset the effects of psychological shock and potential infection from the many wounds sustained prior to, and during, the violent capture process.

Despite the success of their nefarious activities, Griffin's and Goldsberry's actions did not go unchallenged. In addition to the public outcry occasioned by the 1970 Penn Cove capture, in which four calves and a mother drowned, protestors gathered outside the Seattle Marine Aquarium to voice their dissent. Among others, Progressive Animal Welfare Society (PAWS), based in Lynnwood, Seattle, posted notices declaring that "all persons interested in protesting inhumane treatment of WHALES meet at PIER 56 12 Noon Saturday August 22."

In addition to Lolita, the other orcas captured with her, namely Lil Nooka, Chappy, Jumbo, Clovis, Ramu III, Ramu IV and an orphaned calf (Whale), another victim of the hunt who stranded on Bainbridge Island near Seattle, awaited their fate. Following some basic training to prepare them for their lives as entertainers, the whales were dispatched to their new homes. Lil Nooka's future home was Sea-Arama Marineworld, Galveston, Texas; Chappy and Jumbo were sent to Kamagowa Sea World, Japan; Clovis went to Marineland, Antibes, France; Ramu III (later renamed Winston) went to Windsor Safari Park, Berkshire, England; Ramu IV's destination was Marineland of Australia; and Whale (also known as Wally) was sold to Munich Aquarium, Germany.

Marine mammal veterinarian Dr. Jesse White (1935–1996) was allocated the task of selecting a suitable whale to join Hugo, another Southern Resident captured as a three-year-old in Vaughn Bay, Tacoma, in February 1968 and already incarcerated at the Miami Seaquarium.

The Seaquarium, one of the oldest oceanariums in the United States, was founded in 1955 by Captain W.B. Gray and Fred D. Coppock and funded by Marine Exhibition Corporation (which formed its Florida corporation on December 7, 1953) on land leased from Miami-Dade County. The complex sits on a small man-made island between Key Biscayne and the mainland, which is accessed by the Rickenbacker Causeway. In 1960, the park was acquired by Wometco Enterprises, the shortened name for the Wolfson-Meyer Theater Company, founded in 1925 by brothers-in-law Mitchell Wolfson and Sidney Meyer. The main attraction at that time was the Golden Dome Sea Lion Stadium. The Flipper Lagoon became the location for the making of a well-known popular American television program starring Flipper, a bottlenose dolphin. Eighty-eight episodes of *Flipper* were filmed between 1964 and 1967 by Ivan Tors, the cinematographer who filmed the live capture of Shamu—a member of J pod and the second Southern Resident to be captured—and co-produced the film *Namu: The Killer Whale* in conjunction with Metro-Goldwyn-Mayer Television. Two movies starring Flipper were also filmed there.

Arthur Herman Hertz (1933–2017) former chief executive officer of Wometco Enterprises and the Miami Seaquarium, graduated from the University of Miami in 1955 with a bachelor of arts degree. He joined Wometco as an accountant in 1956 and was appointed to the position of controller in 1960. In 1964, he became vice president and was later promoted to senior vice president; he was elected to the position of director in 1971.

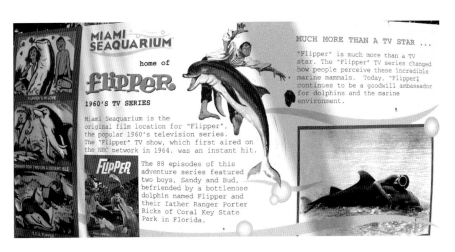

Flipper exhibit at the Miami Seaquarium. *Ingrid N. Visser, Orca Research Trust.*

Johnson, Francis P. Miami's Seaquarium, 1955. Black & white photoprint, 4 x 5 in. *State Archives of Florida, Florida Memory.*

In 1981, he became executive vice president and treasurer, rising to chief financial officer in 1983. After Wometco Enterprises Inc. was purchased by a group of private investors headed by Kohlberg Kravis Roberts & Co., Hertz scraped together $60 million and bought many of Kohlberg Kravis Roberts's entertainment assets. Three years later, he bought rights to the Wometco name and took up the position of chairman and chief executive officer of Wometco Enterprises.[1]

In time, the company, which at one point had as many as twenty-eight different franchises and owned half a dozen television stations—including WTVJ (TV-6, Miami), a National Broadcasting Company owned and operated television station—sold its empire of movie theaters but continued to run the Seaquarium.

According to Dr. White's daughter Lisa, White described Lolita as "so courageous and yet so gentle" and named her Tokitae after visiting a curio shop in Seattle, where he spotted the name on a carving. The cultural meaning of the name derives from a Coast Salish greeting meaning "nice day, pretty colors," and was used when members of different tribes who dwelt along the shores of the Salish Sea rivers met one another while traveling or trading.

At that time, orcas were selling for $20,000 each. A $10,000 deposit was put down for Tokitae (Lolita), the remaining $10,000 to be paid on safe delivery to the Seaquarium.

A couple of months later, the *Miami News* reported that Tokitae was now officially known as Lolita, the name given to the precocious heroine of Russian writer Vladimir Nabokov's novel of the same title. Jane Wrigley, who dealt with the Seaquarium's publicity, referred to Tokitae as a "screaming Lolita," and that became her name.[2] It was more in keeping with the flashy Miami showbiz image and would help to avoid unwelcome questions about her true origins. It was a cruel coincidence that Nabokov had conceived the idea for the book after reading a newspaper story about a captive ape that—after months of coaxing—produced the first ever charcoal drawing done by an animal depicting the bars of the poor creature's cage.

After encasement in a canvas sling, Lolita was once again hoisted by crane from the Seattle Marine Aquarium and lowered to a flatbed truck for transportation to Seattle-Tacoma International Airport. From there, she would be transferred to an aircraft for the 2,724-mile flight to Miami International Airport. The days of traveling with her pod exploring the ancient waterways of her cultural heritage were over. Soon the cooling currents of the Pacific Ocean would be replaced by filtered water from the Bay of Biscayne. Every day, she would suffer the humidity and scorching heat of the relentless Miami sun. There would be no more joyous breaching against the backdrop of the glacial peaks and snow-capped mountain ranges that form much of the Pacific Northwest's magnificent landscape. Instead, she would learn to jump on cue for a meal of dead fish, with a fleeting glimpse of the galaxy beyond flaking concrete bleachers and a corrugated metal roof. The scream of jets flying directly overhead to and from Miami International Airport and the constant rumble of traffic would assail her senses. Although the ocean—and freedom—beckoned nearby, she could no longer see the place she knew as home. Now her future lay in serving her masters, Wometco Enterprises. In just a few short weeks, like many other members of her extended family, she had become just another commodity.

2

HUGO AND LOLITA

On arrival at the Miami Seaquarium on September 24, 1970, the little whale described as "Lolita—the sloe-eyed beauty…a lady killer whale selected to be the bride of Hugo, the handsome boy killer whale now cavorting in his big new tank," was once again "walked" around her new tank and injected with antibiotics.[3]

The average September temperature in Miami is around 88 degrees Fahrenheit, but there was no shelter for Lolita from the harsh, penetrating rays of the blazing sun. Pat Sykes, one of three women hired to be a show assistant, or "Aquamaid," at the Miami Seaquarium from June 1970 to August 1973, recalled Lolita's arrival. "She [Lolita] had a very hard time—she just barely floated. The skin on her back cracked and bled from the sun and wind exposure. She wouldn't eat the diet of frozen herring. At night she cried."

Sykes, who later became one of the petitioners requesting National Oceanic and Atmospheric Administration (NOAA) Fisheries to include Lolita under the 1973 Endangered Species Act (ESA) listing of the Southern Residents, wrote in a personal memo to Berta and Garrett that Lolita was so traumatized she did not swim or eat for days. Sykes's father, a maintenance worker at the Seaquarium, rigged up a temporary sun shelter for Lolita, and he rubbed lanolin on her back. Sykes found Lolita easy to work with and exceptionally trusting.

Lolita spent the first eight months of her new life in the "celebrity pool" (now the manatee tank) comprising two small pools thirty-five feet in diameter

Patty Sykes performs with a killer whale at Miami's Seaquarium, 1973. Black & white photoprint, 4 x 5 in. *State Archives of Florida, Florida Memory.*

containing eighty thousand gallons of water. It was here, since his arrival in May 1968, that Hugo spent the first two years of his life with a Pacific white-sided dolphin for company. Former Flipper dolphin trainer turned anti-captivity activist Ric O'Barry said, "When I fed Hugo, his tail would be lying on the bottom and his head would be completely out of the water. It was pathetic. They wanted me to train him. I refused and left in disgust."

Construction of the new whale tank (commonly referred to as the "Whale Bowl"), designed by architect A. Herbert Mathes, complete with a roofed stadium to seat two thousand people, began in November 1969 and is believed to have cost around $750,000. Construction of the back part of the tank, known as the "medical pool," commenced in 1974 and was completed the following year. Hugo's scheduled move from the celebrity pool to the Whale Bowl in June 1970 was threatened by a plumber's strike amid other concerns that he would outgrow the celebrity pool. Since his arrival at the Seaquarium, the young male had grown four and a half feet and gained almost one ton in weight.[4]

Both Lolita and Hugo were members of L pod, although that fact was unknown at the time. It was not until Dr. Michael A. Bigg (1939–1990), a Canadian researcher with the Fisheries Research Board of Canada Biological Station, Nanaimo, British Columbia, began his groundbreaking photo-identification study of killer whales in the early 1970s that a picture of distinct populations and orca cultures began to emerge.

Following her introduction to her new home, Lolita and Hugo were initially kept apart, as it was feared they might fight. Up until June 1971, when Lolita was transferred to the Whale Bowl, the pair communicated over the air with an array of high-pitched squeals and whistles—the unique vocalizations of L pod. Sykes described how, when Hugo heard Lolita's vocalizations, he whistled back and swam around the tank faster and faster, smashing his rostrum into the Plexiglass window. When Sykes reported Hugo's behavior, she was dismissed as being a "flannel-headed eighteen-year-old" with the words "he will never break it."

But break it he did, crashing into the five-foot-diameter plastic bubble projecting twenty inches into the tank and knocking a nine-inch hole in it. A jagged piece of plastic severed the front of his rostrum (the tip of a whale's head), while a 510,000-gallon rush of chemically treated refrigerated water gushed over his blowhole.

The water level in the tank was dropped immediately to enable recovery of the two-inch piece of severed flesh, which Dr. White sewed back on an hour and a half later. Although the veterinarian attempted to give Hugo a local anesthetic, the large hypodermic syringe could not penetrate the whale's thick skin. Forty steel stitches were inserted, with Hugo remaining calm throughout the procedure. Within a week, the flap of skin turned white, and it fell off when the stitches were removed. The tissue underneath had begun to granulate and heal, and six months later, Hugo had a new rostrum.[5]

On the day Lolita was to be transferred to the Whale Bowl, manager Burton Clark, announced, "We're putting Lolita into the tank early this morning but separating the two by bulkheads," adding that once Hugo gave some indication of his intentions, the Seaquarium would unite the pair. The operation was expected to take three hours. Starting at 8:00 a.m., the 3,400-pound Lolita was lifted by crane and slowly maneuvered into the smaller section of the tank.[6]

No one knew how Hugo would react to Lolita's presence. In fact, introducing the two orcas to each other created an unexpected social hierarchy. A week after Lolita joined him, Hugo began to show a change of personality, becoming moody and withdrawn. In late July, the press reported that "life with Lolita has turned fat and happy Hugo into a toothy, two-ton terror."[7] Anthony G. Toran, administrative director of the Seaquarium, said that Hugo had, on at least a dozen occasions, vented his frustrations on staff. The juvenile male grabbed hold of a trainer's raincoat and shouldered another trainer against a side of the tank with the full force of his substantial bulk. Hugo also terrified some of the female performers by sneaking up behind them, snapping his jaws and lunging half his full length up onto the slide-out barrier between the main tank and the medical pool.

In an effort to contain Hugo's aggressive tendencies, his diet and training methods were changed. But with no sign of improvement in his behavior, his performances were canceled, and he was temporarily retired. Lolita would be trained to replace him.[8]

A year later, trainer Manny Velasco was posing for the cameras with his head in Lolita's mouth, pandering to a thrill-seeking public. Velasco and another trainer, Mike Jacques, both said they preferred working with Lolita. The controlled power of her sleek, streamlined body breaking the surface and arcing mid-air before cleanly re-entering the shallow twenty-foot depth of the tank drew the crowds and boosted ticket sales. Nobody asked where she came from. Nobody cared.

The tank, which is not big enough for one orca, let alone two, has been the subject of contention for many years. But here, until his death of a brain aneurysm in 1980, Hugo and Lolita performed together up to four times a day. Sykes said that they both had to work hard for their keep, and that if they did not perform to Velasco's increasingly "bizarre" conditions, he deprived them of food. When Sykes complained about his behavior, she was told it was a personality issue—hers. After seeing Velasco short-change the whales one more time, Sykes fed Lolita her entire bucket of fish and walked out the door. She never went back.

Despite Lolita being too young to conceive by the standards of the time (today orcas in captivity as young as seven years old are reproducing) and no killer whale had, as far as was known, conceived or borne calves in captivity, the Seaquarium had high hopes that Lolita and Hugo would produce live offspring. In October 1972, they enlisted the assistance of psychic Marlowe Gray to determine if Lolita was pregnant. Wearing a Hindu cloak and jeweled turban, Gray (who claimed to be able to tell if a woman was pregnant by psychic vibrations—it transpired that the woman he was referring to was his first wife), climbed down a ladder to commune with Lolita. He announced that Lolita was not pregnant but that she would become so in the week

Nilson, Stig. Animal trainer performing with an Orca whale at the Miami Seaquarium attraction, 1983. Color slide. *State Archives of Florida, Florida Memory.*

Hugo and Lolita. View showing orca whales leaping out of the water for animal trainers during a show at the Miami Seaquarium attraction, no date. Color slide. *State Archives of Florida, Florida Memory.*

starting on May 16 (1973), saying, "I cleared my mind before I went down the ladder and opened myself up to the vibrations of the whale."[9]

The gestation period for orcas is seventeen or eighteen months. In December 1975, it was announced that although Hugo and Lolita had been observed mating, Gray's prediction proved incorrect.

The awakening of the whales' sexual appetites was causing some problems for trainers Chip Kirk and Bob Pulaski. At times, both Hugo and Lolita refused to perform. On one occasion, Hugo would not let Kirk leave the tank. "He kept pushing me around. See the scar on my arm. That's where he grabbed me. He sort of chewed playfully, like a dog will."

Pulaski also experienced some unwelcome attention from Hugo during an unguarded moment when Hugo grabbed the trainer by his wetsuit and shook him. Orcas, with their high intelligence and social bonding, work as a team. Despite her docile nature, Lolita was still a wild creature trapped in an alien environment. Heeding her natural instincts, she joined Hugo in the game, and between them, the pair tore off Pulaski's wetsuit.[10]

In spite of the dangers, head trainer John Scanlon, who worked with the whales six hours a day, was keen to teach Hugo a new trick in addition to the twenty or so that he and Lolita already knew. Prying open Hugo's mouth, Scanlon placed himself between Hugo's two rows of three-inch-long, razor-sharp teeth while Hugo lifted him out of the water. "Hugo doesn't seem to like this stunt," Scanlon said. "Sometimes when I force myself into his mouth, he trembles. It's like he's afraid he might hurt me."[11]

Perhaps the trainers thought that playing soothing music to the whales would be appreciated. American songwriter, singer and actor Jim Turner, who has national credits from radio, television and Broadway, serenaded Hugo and Lolita with Bach sonatas on his musical saw.

After ten years of performing together, Hugo and Lolita were destined to be split apart when, on March 4, 1980, Hugo, who had been acting sluggish since mid-January, was found dead at the bottom of the tank. He was around fifteen years of age, a sprouter (teenage) male who should have been in the prime of his life. Although he and Lolita had been given three days off from performing in 1977 in the hope that Lolita might conceive, Hugo died without offspring. After twelve years of entertaining the public and serving a corporation, his carcass was reputedly removed to the Miami-Dade landfill for disposal. Nothing but memories marked his passing.[12]

Following Hugo's death, it was business as usual for Wometco Enterprises, which wasted no time in changing its advertisements and brochures featuring Hugo and Lolita together. When asked about Lolita's reaction to the death of her companion, Warren Zeiller, manager of the Seaquarium, said that Lolita was "doing beautifully" and taking the loss in stride. Former trainer Eric Eimstad (now general manager of the Seaquarium) stated that although staff had found Lolita bumping up against Hugo's body, she hadn't shown any outward signs of grieving and continued with her performance the following day. He told the press that a new show was in the planning stage and that Lolita could do everything Hugo had been able to do. As he put it, "It's up to her to carry on."[13]

Despite Eimstad's assertion that Lolita was taking the loss of Hugo in stride, a study conducted in 1986 on killer whale behavior featuring both Hugo and Lolita (referred to in the study as Tokitae, nickname Toki) states: "After the death of Hugo, Toki would briefly surface to catch a breath, then would return to the bottom to continue her long bouts of submerged floating. Before the loss of Hugo, she usually remained at the surface for prolonged periods, breathing successively while floating there." The study goes on to say that "certainly, the activity pattern which emerged for Toki subsequent to Hugo's death is not unlike bereavement."[14]

Four months later, visitors to the Seaquarium were paying admission fees of six dollars for adults and three dollars for children to watch Lolita floating on her back while a trainer and dolphin hopped onto her stomach.[15] Because of her prowess in performing a stunt with a dolphin riding her piggyback, a year later, Lolita starred in the TV show *That's Incredible*. Notwithstanding her popularity, she did not always cooperate. When she failed to leap twenty feet into the air and flip three times on cue, Eimstad turned his back on her and walked away as a punishment. Speaking of Lolita's disposition, he said, "She's gotten mad before, she's snapped, but never at anyone."[16]

By October 1981, Lou Roth, Lolita's then trainer, boasted that Lolita could perform twenty-one "behaviors," or tricks, and knew forty altogether.[17] He added that although the Seaquarium would like to get a mate for her, to purchase and train another killer whale would cost in the region of $175,000. Since the last capture of killer whales in Washington State in March 1976, prohibitions against capturing whales in U.S. waters and new standards for tanks now made obtaining killer whales from the wild much more difficult.

With Hugo gone, Lolita would remain mostly alone, except for the company of Pacific white-sided dolphins and, in December 1989, a three-and-a-half-year-old, thirteen-foot male long-finned pilot whale named Cookie (also known as Christmas Cookie). He was one of thirty-eight whales

Cookie and Lolita. *Orca Network.*

Ric O'Barry with Hugo in 1969. "I was his trainer. I survived that experience. Hugo did not. Lolita does not have to die there like Hugo. She can be returned to her home range to retire. If only the greedy bastards who exploit her had a heart." *Dolphin Project.com.*

that stranded in Massachusetts, New England, on Christmas Day 1986 and had outgrown his tank at Sealand of Cape Cod.

Initially, as when Lolita was moved from the celebrity pool to join Hugo, the two whales were separated by bulkheads. The reaction of both whales to the presence of the other was one of equal curiosity. Lolita and Makani, one of the Pacific white-sided dolphins, tried to raise themselves high enough to see over the barriers along with similar attempts by the pilot whale. At one point, Makani jumped the barrier and sped around the tank while Cookie and his companion, a saddleback dolphin (also known as a short-beaked common dolphin) who had shared the tank at Sealand, cowered in a corner. When the barrier was removed, the metal tube gates stayed open so that Cookie could join Lolita. The pilot whale tentatively swam toward her, whereupon Lolita turned away. Despite several attempts to integrate the two whales, Lolita remained aloof. On one occasion, she circled the tank at high speed while Cookie, emitting frightened high-pitched squeaks, once again attempted to take refuge.[18] When Cookie died in July 1994, O'Barry said he should have been released long ago. "There's only three things that kill dolphins—our nets, our pollution, and our captivity," O'Barry stated. "Their behavior is so radically altered by their habitat that they no longer represent dolphins and whales in nature. It's nothing more than a display of dominance."

3

BRING LOLITA HOME

Following public pressure over the highly publicized 1970 Penn Cove capture, the Washington State legislature passed a law in August 1971 requiring that permits be obtained to capture killer whales. Payment of $1,000 was required for each whale captured and a limit put on the number of whales per capture. Along with the inception of the Marine Mammal Protection Act (MMPA) in December 1972, although orcas now received some degree of protection, they remained vulnerable to exploitation.

In addition to the efforts made to regulate killer whale hunting, in 1971, Bigg conducted the first of a three-year census in Canada, Washington State and Alaska. The results showed that the number of whales was alarmingly low, a far cry from the common perception that there were hundreds of them. Not only that, but Bigg's pioneering photo-identification studies of the dorsal fins and saddle patches of individual whales displaying their unique markings revealed that the same whales were repeatedly being rounded up.

Across the border in Washington State, in order to establish whether Bigg was correct in his estimation of the killer whale population, whale researcher Kenneth C. Balcomb III began his Orca Survey in April 1976, a month after the last capture near Olympia. Balcomb contracted with National Marine Fisheries Service (NMFS) to conduct a six-month study of the remaining Southern Residents, which, after ten years of "cropping," totaled seventy-one. Prior to the captures, the number exceeded one hundred whales.

Balcomb's first log entry on April 1 makes interesting reading, in particular regarding the reception that greeted the team when they moored

Ken Balcomb with Fluke (L102) and mother Racer (L72). *Richard Snowberger.*

for the night in Port Townsend on the Olympic Peninsula. After walking into town for dinner and a few beers, Balcomb and his crew handed out information about the survey to interested parties. Although the group was mostly well received, some people expressed concern as to which side Balcomb was on. During their first encounter with approximately forty whales on April 8, there was also skepticism on the whales' side. Balcomb wrote, "It was very apparent that the whales were initially concerned with avoiding us." Although the whales eventually settled down, when Balcomb later approached a female orca with double notch scars on her dorsal fin, he reported that "she was not at ease with our presence. Did she get her scars from man?" Among the whales photographed that day was Ocean Sun.

In the summer of that year, Balcomb's younger half brother Howard Garrett joined him on San Juan Island. Here Garrett enjoyed his first encounter with whales and, more specifically, the Southern Resident orcas. After watching two orcas swimming close to each other with a baby harbor porpoise—which they playfully flipped into the air a few times—tucked in between them (although traditionally fish eaters, Southern Residents have been observed on occasion to adopt this behavior), Garrett said, "I felt like I was on another planet." The memorable encounter would stay etched in Garrett's mind forever and was the prelude to his lifelong dedication to whales. He also discovered that there was just one survivor from the Washington State capture era—Lolita. Hearing her torrid story, that first

Howard Garrett (*left*) and Ken Balcomb hitching a ride. *Ken Balcomb.*

summer, within sight and sound of her family, was the launch pad for Garrett's rollercoaster journey to bring her home.

Born in Albuquerque, New Mexico, on December 27, 1945, one of two sons of an Air Force pilot, Robert Garrett and his wife, Barbara, a professional musician, Garrett had had a somewhat checkered career. After commencing his studies for a sociology degree in 1963 at the University of New Mexico, he transferred to the University of California at Berkeley. Garrett chose not to complete his degree at the time, opting to avoid the draft by working on dairy farms in Scotland, Germany and Canada.

After spotting a short article in the nationwide Sunday newspaper magazine *Parade* and learning that President Richard Milhous Nixon (R) (1913–1994), in office from January 1969 to August 1974 and the only U.S. president to resign, had dropped seventy-two thousand federal cases against draft dodgers, Garrett's stepmother contacted the Federal Bureau of Investigation (FBI). The agency confirmed that Garrett's case was among those listed. On receiving a postcard from his stepmother telling him that he could return to his country without fear of reprisal, in July 1972, Garrett traveled back to his homeland. He and two friends purchased fifty acres of land in New Mexico, intending to build, and live in, a commune-style setting. He married in 1973, and his son was born a year later. The couple eventually divorced.

Garrett resumed his sociology degree at Colorado College in 1979, supporting himself by volunteering on the graveyard shift on a crisis hotline and working as an orderly on a hospital psychiatric ward.[19]

After completing his degree in 1980, he moved to San Juan Island to help Balcomb run the Whale Museum in Friday Harbor. The museum was based in a building originally known as the Odd Fellows Hall, which Balcomb rented from Emilia Lee Bave (1910–2008) for $75 a month. Here Garrett worked as an administrator editing the magazine *Cetus* and also found himself cast in the unexpected role of American settler Lyman Cutler in Bave's theatrical rendition of the Pig War whenever she could round up an audience. The fifteen-year-long war (1859–74) sparked between Britain and America after Cutler shot and killed a wandering pig suffered only one casualty—the pig. The dispute created over ownership of the San Juan Islands was peacefully resolved by arbitration through Kaiser Wilhelm I of Germany, who ruled in favor of the United States.

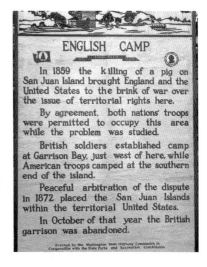

The Pig War. *Author collection.*

In addition to assisting Balcomb at the Whale Museum, Garrett became involved in Orca Survey. He now found himself exposed to an intense whale-oriented society and almost daily encounters with the Southern Residents. Being in proximity to these iconic creatures stirred a passion within him to learn more about this culturally distinct society of whales whose future was, and remains, so uncertain. Garrett's involvement took the pressure off Balcomb, leaving him free to spend more time studying orca demographics. In 1985, Balcomb formed the Center for Whale Research, of which he remains the executive director and principal researcher.

Garrett's frequent encounters with the Southern Resident orcas also fueled a fire within him to protect this embattled species. When Sealand of the Pacific, Victoria, British Columbia, obtained a special permit to capture two killer whales in 1982, despite the provincial government having prohibited further live captures in 1975, Garrett camped out along the shore of Pedder Bay, British Columbia, in late August with other American and Canadian environmentalists, including Greenpeace, to monitor and oppose any capture. Sealand officials hoped that one of the Southern Resident pods (L pod, according to the April 1983 edition of the *Barklay Sounder*) would return, as whales had been spotted in the area within the last few days. Greenpeace officials announced that they planned to disrupt the capture by banging pipes and oars on the side of boats to create a disturbance similar to the methods used in Taiji, Japan, to drive dolphins into a cove, thus preventing the orcas from entering the bay. "If the whales do get caught, we will try to free them," said Patrick Moore, director of Greenpeace Canada. Although no capture took place on this occasion, it was Garrett's first foray into activism for whales—but by no means his last.

Part of Lolita's family traveling in harmony. *Richard Snowberger.*

Greenpeace was on the ground again in March 1983 when, according to a spokesperson, a further plan was underway to capture whales under the permit in the vicinity of Barklay Sound, British Columbia, where the M/V *Western Spray* was waiting near Tzartus Island. Should any orcas venture into the area, the vessel would endeavor to head them into waiting nets. In the event of the attempt being successful, Bigg would be asked to identify the pod. If it was L pod, the largest pod, Lolita's family would lose two more members. Fortunately, no capture was made. Faced with constant opposition from activists, Bob Wright, owner of Sealand of the Pacific, eventually gave up and purchased three orcas from Iceland.

While Bigg and Balcomb continued with their photo-identification studies, Dr. John Ford's research results on dialects within whale communities were emerging. As a sociology major studying communications and cultural transmission, Garrett was interested in Ford's scientific findings. Ford, whose career path began as a whale trainer at the Vancouver Aquarium, British Columbia, progressed to the position of marine mammal curator/scientist before he joined Canada's Department of Fisheries and Oceans (DFO) in 2001.

In addition to helping his brother, Garrett worked as a naturalist on whale-watching boats in the San Juan Islands before joining a research boat in the Caribbean to study humpback whales. When the vessel returned to its home port in Gloucester, Massachusetts, Garrett obtained a further position as naturalist where he remained for the next ten years.

During his absence from the Pacific Northwest, in 1991, orcas in captivity commanded a great deal of attention with the unprecedented death of trainer Keltie Byrne in February of that year. Twenty-year-old Byrne was killed by the Icelandic orca Tilikum at Sealand of the Pacific when she fell into the tank. The coroner's inquest ruled that she drowned "due to or as a consequence of forced submersion by orca (killer) whales." Tilikum, captured off Iceland in 1983, had made history of the worst kind. And as so often happens, history tends to repeat itself.

Following his return to San Juan Island, Garrett's life was about to take an unexpected turn when the film *Free Willy*, starring another captive orca, Keiko (originally named Kago), hit the big screen in 1993. In the film, a boy named Jesse befriends an orca called Willy. When he learns that the marine park owner plans to dispose of Willy and claim the insurance, Jesse befriends Willy's trainer and a park grounds man. Between them, the three tow Willy to safety in a specially constructed trailer.

In reality, like Tilikum, two-year-old Keiko was torn from his mother off the coast of Iceland in 1979 by Jon Gunnarson, purportedly for $50,000, and transferred to an aquarium, or private zoo, in southern Iceland. There does not appear to be any documentation of the capture, a practice known as "hiding" (or laundering) whales, when the number of whales captured exceeds the number of permits granted. Keiko was sold to Marineland, Ontario, Canada, sometime between 1980 and 1982; there appears to be no documentation regarding Keiko's purchase or transport to Marineland.[20] Here he was housed in a sunless warehouse known as the Barn, where he was left to wallow in a shallow pool away from public view. Another Icelandic whale, Junior, captured in 1984 and kept in Saedyrasafnid, Iceland, until December 1986 prior to transfer to Marineland, died in the Barn in July 1994 after five years of mostly solitary confinement. His crime? He was dominated by other orcas and did not respond well to training.

Keiko first appeared before the public in 1982, the youngest of six orcas performing at Marineland, and the least self-confident. He was picked on by an older female and developed lesions (papilloma), a skin condition similar to warts in appearance. In 1985, he was sold for $350,000 to Reino Aventura (Adventure Kingdom), an amusement park in Mexico City, where his health gradually deteriorated.

Following Warner Bros.'s release of *Free Willy* in July 1993, millions of schoolchildren around the world took a personal interest in Keiko and his living conditions. This prompted the film's producers, Richard "Dick" Donner, director of *Superman*, and his wife, Lauren Schuler-Donner, who lived on Orcas Island (part of the San Juan archipelago), together with Reino Aventura and animal protection advocates to try to find Keiko a new home. The movie's massive success nurtured the idea that captive orcas could be successfully released—a piece of unwelcome news for the marine park industry. Although no captive killer whales had been released back to the wild, in 1967, Bimbo, a pilot whale captured in 1959 by Frank Brocata, head of animal collections at Marineland of the Pacific, Los Angeles, California, was released close to the original capture site near Catalina Channel, California. He was deemed a risk to the public after breaking through the glass of the tank. Bimbo was sighted in California waters in 1969 and 1974.

With widespread interest in Keiko's future, in May 1993, the Donners relayed a request to Balcomb to help formulate a plan for Keiko's potential release. The project necessitated a six-to-twelve-month commitment, during which time Garrett dealt with the onslaught of media inquiries bombarding the Center for Whale Research. The small volunteer organization became the catalyst of an international campaign, with a constant flow of phone calls and faxes, plus requests for radio and television interviews.

Although Balcomb's meticulously researched plan for Keiko's rehabilitation and release was later rejected (he was dropped from the project after SeaWorld was informed about it), his valuable study into how to release a captive orca was not lost. The flurry of publicity surrounding Keiko and Balcomb's involvement drew attention to where Balcomb was based—the Pacific Northwest—once again stirring the memories and controversy surrounding Lolita.

Principally a scientist rather than a sociologist, Balcomb offered the Seaquarium $250,000 to conduct a whale-to-whale acoustic experiment between Lolita and her family. He proposed placing a satellite phone and hydrophones in Lolita's tank and in Haro Strait, where the Southern Residents often roam. Balcomb hoped to monitor both her physical and verbal responses, in particular when she heard her family's vocalizations. He already knew that she vocalized when orca tapes were played, even though they were not of the Southern Resident community. Although it was a robust and novel idea that offered an intriguing study, Arthur Hertz rejected the offer as "bad science."[21]

With tourist numbers and revenue down following Hurricane Andrew's devastating onslaught, which destroyed over twenty-five thousand homes in Miami-Dade alone and damaged hundreds more in August 1992, Hertz was unlikely to cooperate with an experiment that threatened to prove his

Keiko's popularity helps promote shoe sales. *Orca Network.*

biggest asset had a chance of rejoining her family. The Seaquarium had been hit hard by the storm, the most destructive hurricane in the history of the United States to that point, with winds reaching up to 165 miles per hour. A storm tide of four to six feet was measured in Biscayne Bay on August 24, with eight inches of rainfall recorded in Broward and Miami-Dade Counties. Two feet of silty water, full of bay sediment, covered the park. Several sharks and fish died when their pool pumping systems flooded, and five sea lions were electrocuted.[22]

Concerned for Lolita's safety in the event of further hurricane damage, Balcomb wrote to the Seaquarium on September 1, 1992, offering to undertake a fundraising campaign to raise enough money to buy Lolita and transport her to Seattle for eventual reunion with her family. That offer, too, was rejected.

While the grass-roots movement to retire Lolita was gathering strength in Washington State, word spread to Miami. After visiting the Seaquarium, where he says he felt "a sense of unbelievable oppression," and inspired by the film *Free Willy*, media mogul Jerry Powers, publisher of the glossy, up-market fashion magazine *Ocean Drive*, ran a $10,000 "Free Lolita/Boycott Miami Seaquarium" promotion alongside advertisements for top designers such as Hermès and Ralph Lauren. Working with O'Barry, Powers also ran $7,000-a-month billboards for Lolita along Interstate 95, declaring, "Whatever it takes, whatever it costs, we have the money."

The inimitable Powers devoted three years of his life to the campaign, contacting famous celebrities, including musician Sir Elton John and actor Sylvester Stallone. In response to former trainer Marcia Henton's dismissive statement relating to any potential release that it was "ridiculous, she's been under human care for a quarter of a century. She's just not a candidate to be plunked back in the ocean. She wouldn't even survive the trip across the country," Powers retorted, "Oh? Then how did she survive the trip here?"[23]

Powers was successful in procuring a rare interview with Hertz, whom he declared was "all business." Taking pride of place in Hertz's office was a big picture of himself with Lolita, contrasting sharply with a much smaller family photo. Powers had no doubt that Hertz loved Lolita—in the tank. Despite his efforts to persuade Hertz to release her, which included an offer to fund a film of the release, he was dismissed from Hertz's office almost before the meeting was over.

The media mogul was not the only person to be inspired by Keiko's story. The interest of first-time governor Michael Edward Lowry (1939–2017), twentieth governor of the State of Washington (1993–97), was piqued. In July 1994, Lowry attended a meeting on San Juan Island and visited Kanaka Bay, on the west side of the island, where shooting was taking place for *Free Willy* 2. Kanaka Bay also was the location where Pender and Flores, the last two orcas held captive in Washington State in 1976, were transported in preparation for their release. The bay, which lies on the west side of the island and looks across the Strait of Juan de Fuca to the Olympic Peninsula, is within range of where Lolita's family pass by and would later become a potential sea-pen site for her retirement.

On learning of Lowry's presence on the island, Balcomb approached him with a request to write a letter in support of the proposal to bring Lolita home. Lowry seemed to take to the idea but didn't commit to it at the time, passing Balcomb on to Kathy Kelly (known as Kelly), his political aide. Balcomb and Garrett discussed the matter with Kelly, who requested more

Michael Edward Lowry, twentieth governor of the U.S. state of Washington (1993–1997). *Washington State Archives.*

STATE OF WASHINGTON

OFFICE OF THE GOVERNOR

P.O. Box 40002 • Olympia, Washington 98504-0002 • (206) 753-6780

MEDIA ADVISORY

March 6, 1995

Gov. Lowry, Sec. Of State Munro propose releasing Orca whale

Olympia - Gov. Mike Lowry and Secretary of State Ralph Munro will announce a proposal to return Lolita, the last surviving Washington Orca whale still in captivity, to her home in Puget Sound. The announcement will take place at Daybreak Star in Seattle's Discovery Park on Thursday, March 9, at 11 a.m.

Lolita was captured off Whidbey Island in 1970. For the last 25 years she has lived in captivity at a Florida marine park, where she performs two shows a day, 365 days a year. With the Center for Whale Research, Lowry and Munro would like to negotiate the release of Lolita from captivity, her rehabilitation and a return to her native pod, which lives in the Puget Sound.

###

Press release, March 6, 1995. Governor Lowry and Secretary of State Munro propose releasing orca whale (Lolita). *Orca Network.*

background information on the project. A few days later she confirmed it was a viable option but expressed some concern over potential political connotations, in particular the possible condemnation taking such a stance might imply for the three beluga whales held at Point Defiance Zoo and Aquarium in Tacoma, Olympia.

Balcomb and Garrett waited hopefully for a positive outcome. A few months later, in March 1995, Lowry and Munro, who in 1976 played a leading role in the instigation of the lawsuit banning SeaWorld from capturing orcas in Washington State, together with Garrett and Balcomb launched the Tokitae campaign, leading to the formation of the Tokitae Foundation, a 501(c)(3) nonprofit organization registered in Washington State. Lowry and Munro, along with Balcomb, held a press conference at the Daybreak Star Cultural Center, a Native American cultural center situated in Discovery Park, Seattle, announcing the campaign to bring

Lolita home, with Lowry declaring his intention to help Lolita return "as a citizen of the state of Washington."

Actress Linda Evans, who played Krystle Carrington in the popular prime time television soap opera *Dynasty*, donated $5,000 to help launch the campaign. The soap opera star, who had a home in Tacoma, committed to the project after watching a television special about Lolita. "I was transfixed by this beautiful animal's plight," she stated. "I found myself crying. I thought, 'How can we help this animal? Shouldn't she have a chance at a life in the wild?'" Evans claimed that she had tried to arrange a meeting with Hertz, but he refused her request.

Like Powers, Lowry and Munro attempted to appeal to Hertz's better nature by inviting him and Seaquarium trainers for an expenses-paid whale-watching trip to Puget Sound, in the hope that they would appreciate seeing Lolita's family in the wild. Hertz declined the offer, urging Lowry and Munro instead to make a donation toward the U.S. Manatee Halfway House, a $100,000-plus co-sponsored project with the Miami River Marine Group and the Marine Life Preservation Society.

In the same way children rallied to help Keiko, many in Washington State mailed hundreds of letters and colorful drawings to Wometco Enterprises supporting the campaign to bring Lolita home. One child wrote, "We saw Lolita's family today. Please send her home."

In direct contrast, school students in Miami wrote letters in support of Lolita staying where she was. Their reward? An invitation to a free visit to the Seaquarium, where they were treated to a private behavioral session with Lolita and received "a big, wet splash."

While press columnists Erik Lacitis (*Seattle Times*) and Carl Hiassen (*Miami Herald*) sparred over Lolita's possible liberation, Karen Janson, spokeswoman for the Seaquarium, suggested that the Free Lolita campaign was nothing more than a publicity stunt to divert attention from a growing sex scandal surrounding Governor Lowry. Janson announced that Lolita lived in a refrigerated tank "big enough to house two orcas" and that she was not for sale.[24]

One person who remained quietly in the background throughout the growing debacle was Balcomb. It was not his style to enter into verbal badinage or to seek the limelight. While others volubly sought to appeal to Hertz's sensitivities, Balcomb applied his scientific knowledge and expertise to drafting an acceptable alternative to Lolita's confinement at the Seaquarium. In April 1995, he presented the Center for Whale Research's Comprehensive Retirement Plan at the Annual Meeting of the

P.O. BOX 141609
CORAL GABLES, FLORIDA 33114-1609
Telephone: (305) 529-1403
Facsimile: (305) 529-1466

ARTHUR H. HERTZ
Chairman of the Board and
Chief Executive Officer

February 27, 1996

The Honorable Mike Lowry
Governor
State of Washington
P.O. Box 40002
Olympia, WA 98504-0002

The Honorable Ralph Munro
Secretary of State
Office of the Secretary of State
Legislative Building
P.O. Box 40220
Olympia, WA 98504-0220

Dear Governor Lowry and Secretary Munro:

Please excuse my delay in answering your letter. A belated happy new year to you.

Thank you for letting me know of your continued desire to have Lolita relocated to your state. I wish, however, to restate categorically that such a move is not contemplated and indeed, is not an option. The various financial options you discuss are of no interest to us; Lolita is not for sale, as I have stated previously.

Therefore, asking your various state agencies to spend time and resources on selecting a potential "relocation and release site" is an effort in futility. I would not be so presumptuous as to how to advise you to spend taxpayer money. However, given our stated position on this matter, it would appear that any efforts by your state in this regard would simply result in a waste of funds.

Sincerely,

Arthur Hertz

CORPORATE HEADQUARTERS 3195 PONCE DE LEON BOULEVARD CORAL GABLES FLORIDA

"Lolita is not for sale." Letter from Arthur Hertz to Munro and Lowry, February 27, 1996. *Orca Network.*

American Association of Zoos and Aquariums in Seattle. His proposals for Lolita's rehabilitation/release and reunion were based on science and sound reasoning and aimed in brief:

1. *To reach a sensible business agreement with Lolita's owner(s).*
2. *To acclimate Lolita in a natural seawater pen and train her to "gate" to open water.*
3. *To conduct comprehensive DNA, veterinary and physiological studies before, during and after her transition.*
4. *To contribute to science's understanding of returning cetaceans to the wild.*
5. *To see whether she could still recall and respond to native dialect calls.*
6. *To give Lolita the choice of returning to her family or remaining at the sea-pen.*
7. *To check on Lolita's health on occasions by recalling her to the sea-pen.*
8. *To assess if Lolita could pass on trained behaviors to free-ranging whales.*
9. *To raise public awareness about cetaceans and their environment.*

By now, Lolita had been held in captivity for twenty-five years. But if Keiko could be released back to the wild, then why not Lolita?

SPIRIT IN THE WATER

After Reino Aventura donated him to the Free Willy/Keiko Foundation, in January 1996, Keiko was moved from Mexico City to a new $7.3 million rehabilitation facility at the Oregon Coast Aquarium. In the same month, the powerful one-hour documentary *Lolita: Spirit in the Water*, produced and directed by Sharon Howard and Mike Rosen, narrated by the late Kathi Goertzen for KOMO TV, Seattle, went on air. Howard first saw Lolita in 1992, gaining entry to the Seaquarium under the guise of wanting to become a whale trainer.

This poignant film explores the arguments for, and against, Lolita remaining at the Seaquarium or rejoining her family. Henton, who worked with Lolita from 1988 until 1995, proudly recounts how Lolita's life was monitored with a daily full-body examination, including blood tests and fecal and exhalation samples. Lolita was trained to urinate into a bottle on command to assess her potential for reproduction; there was nothing about Lolita's chemistry that they did not know. Henton stated that Lolita was so intelligent that, if she was given a signal she hadn't received for eight years, she would still recognize and act upon it. Given the fact that orcas have excellent memories (better even than elephants) and a brain four times bigger than the human brain, many would argue that is hardly surprising.

Henton also revealed that Lolita was a picky eater, spitting out salmon if the heads were not removed (Garrett believes that her refusal to eat unless the fish is cut up just right may be a way of maintaining some control over her situation.) Her diet of frozen fish, which is brought out in an

Keiko arrives in Oregon. *Orca Network*.

ice bucket and tossed into her mouth as a reward, consists of a mix of salmon, smelt and herring. Seaquarium staff claim that she is terrified of live grouper—or perhaps she is simply not interested in it. Southern Residents rely on a diet of Chinook salmon, with chum and Coho salmon their second choices. Grouper does not constitute part of their traditional diet, nor as Eimstad claimed when talking about Lolita in 1981, does she eat "sea lions and other whales."

Among those interviewed for the film were Seaquarium curator Robert Rose and former SeaWorld research director Dr. John Hall, who claims that Lolita was showing signs of stress and becoming more aggressive. In his opinion, she was an ideal candidate for release, but the Seaquarium was afraid of setting a precedent. If one killer whale could be successfully released, why not others? Hall also said, although there had been talk of a new tank for twenty years, he suspected that in twenty years' time, there would still be no new tank.

When asked if he thought Lolita's tank was big enough, veterinarian Dr. Michael Renner said he did not have the dimensions but he would have thought so, adding that Lolita had educated, and would continue to educate, the public about orcas.

O'Barry gave the most damning verdict of all. As he put it, people were being taught that it was all right to use whales for entertainment. Consumers needed to be aware that they were witnessing nothing more than a show of dominance. It was all about money and jobs, supply and demand.

White, the veterinarian who selected Lolita for the Miami Seaquarium in 1970, believed that Lolita should either have a mate or be released.

Lolita's capturer, Griffin, was also interviewed. Howard later revealed that, after she tracked him down, he agreed to meet her in a parking lot at 1:00 a.m. He insisted on having full control over the interview, saying, "Don't change a thing." At the end, he broke down in tears. But these were not tears of remorse for the part he played in capturing and killing whales for profit; they reflected only regret that he could not turn the clock back and do it all over again.

Balcomb reiterated his wish to set up a satellite communication between Lolita and her family, and spoke of the proposal to return Lolita to her home waters. He made it quite clear there was no intention of callously abandoning her in the ocean and that any rehabilitation and/or release to a sea-pen would be conducted with the utmost preparation and care.

One person who did not appear in the documentary was Hertz. The filmmakers' request for an interview was denied.

The documentary's release sparked the founding of Lolita's Legion. The alliance of orca-loving third graders from Hillcrest Elementary School, Oak Harbor, Whidbey Island, was created under the Giraffe Project, an organization promoting civic service. The children drew pictures and wrote letters to federal and state lawmakers, as well as to Hertz, expressing their wish to see Lolita freed and sang along to a new song titled "Lolita Come Home." They also wrote to Island County commissioners whose offices were in Coupeville, overlooking Penn Cove, and who supported the proposal for Lolita's return. Their example sparked a worldwide network of concerned school-aged letter-writers, from Whidbey Island to Australia.

In late July 1995, dolphin trainer turned activist Russ Rector, founder/director of Dolphin Freedom Foundation, received a couple of anonymous calls from Seaquarium employees asking him to look under the whale stadium, which they feared might collapse.

Rector acceded to the request and was disturbed by what he saw. The stadium's grandstand was supported by temporary construction columns, normally used for short-term support while building projects are underway. Water poured through cracks in the cement barely three feet from boxes

Free Lolita. Lolita's legion. *Orca Network.*

marked "Danger, High Voltage." Rusting equipment was scattered on the ground, and electrical cords were wrapped around columns.

Rector filed complaints with Occupational Safety and Health Administration (OSHA), Dade County Fire Department and Dade County's Building and Zoning Code Enforcement Division. He also contacted Animal and Plant Health Inspection Service (APHIS), an agency of the U.S. Department of Agriculture (USDA), the body responsible for inspecting the tank and issuing the Seaquarium's license. According to *Miami New Times*, Hertz admitted in an interview with *Miami Herald* in 1991 that the "Seaquarium is tired…we've got to rebuild."[25]

Despite Rector's efforts to draw attention to the alleged defects, his concerns went unheeded, except for one influential person. After watching Rector's video, shampoo magnate John Paul Jones DeJoria, co-founder and chief executive of John Paul Mitchell Systems, asked the company's Miami distributorship to halt its corporate support of the Seaquarium. DeJoria and Mitchell had built their highly successful business by making cruelty-free hair products. "We were pretty appalled," said Roz Rubenstein, vice president for public relations. "John Paul was taken aback and troubled.… It's decaying, it's rusty, it's cracked. It feels like the animal is being housed there just to make money." Linda Martens of Elite Salon Systems, Miami's Paul Mitchell Systems' distributor that provided free shampoo for the Seaquarium's trainers, sent a fax asking the Seaquarium to stop using the Paul Mitchell Systems' corporate logo on the park's brochures, adding, "I sincerely hope your operation will improve or close down."

One of the key factors in Balcomb's retirement plan for Lolita was to see whether she could still recall and respond to her native dialect calls. In an effort to establish an answer to this question, in May 1996, Canadian broadcaster Keith Henderson, *Dateline NBC*, entered the Seaquarium, ostensibly to interview trainers. Once inside, he played a tape of Lolita's family recorded by Balcomb in July 1995 in Haro Strait during a superpod event. A superpod is when all three pods from the Southern Resident community gather together and engage in a ritualistic greeting ceremony with intense socializing and interaction between the pods. Garrett described the rarely witnessed behavior, which is believed to be unique to Southern Residents: "The pods meet and line up facing each other so it's a big triangle, a couple hundred yards between them. For a short while they hold that formation at the surface.…The formation dissolves…groups pop up…lots of heavy breathing…lots of calls and horseplay. It seems like a very happy time for them." When she heard her family's vocalizations, Lolita responded by intently leaning toward the sound. In Garrett's own words, "She literally leaned over so her ear was as close as she could get it." Henderson did not request permission to play the tape, and not surprisingly, the camera crew was asked to leave the Seaquarium.

Balcomb told *Dateline* that he wanted to retire Lolita from show business and "bring her to a place where she'll be taken care of, and facilitate, if she wants, her return to her family." When asked what could be learned from Lolita that might not already be known, Balcomb replied, "We're going to be able to look into the memory and mind of a whale like we've never had an opportunity before."

The Seaquarium's consulting veterinarian, Dr. Gregory Bossart, viewed Lolita's possible release differently, saying, "To consider her for release is unethical, irresponsible and inhumane." In response to a letter from Betty Albertine of Long Island, Bossart replied that Lolita was accustomed to being hand-fed 180 to 200 pounds of human-quality fish daily and had lost her ability to hunt for live fish. He claimed to have done informal experiments playing killer whale recordings and pop music to Lolita, to which her response had been "mild curiosity."[26]

Despite the negative output from the Seaquarium, Friday Harbor Port Commissioner Brian Calvert, acting on behalf of Representative Jack Metcalf (R-WA-2), endeavored to negotiate with Hertz, who, in late August, agreed to look over Balcomb's proposal and meet with a delegation from Washington State. The proposal and plan were sent to Hertz on October 7, 1996, setting out that, in view of Lolita's age, her performing days were probably almost over and she would be better off back in her home waters. It was pointed out to Hertz that he could become the hero of the day and provide the Seaquarium with millions of dollars in free publicity by retiring Lolita. However, it was not to be—Hertz, whose son Andrew had joined him and was working in the marketing department, canceled the appointment scheduled with Munro, Calvert and Lowry's aide, Kelly, saying that he was afraid of being misquoted. Shortly afterward, Balcomb was refused admission to the Seaquarium.

One idea explored by the Tokitae Foundation was that of returning Lolita to Penn Cove, a proposal that did not meet with wholehearted support in the community. The foundation suspended its request for permission to bring Lolita back to Coupeville after a number of residents hired a lawyer to block any attempt to move her there. They contended that her presence would affect water quality, and the town was too small to cope with the potential traffic intake that might be created by an increase in tourists and

Ralph Munro prepares to lay commemorative flowers honoring the captured whales.
Orca Network.

media attention. Other people supported the idea as a way of healing the community's trauma in the wake of the horrific 1970 capture. "There are so many people who remember the whale capture. There are some human needs here, too," stated one resident.

One way of attempting to heal some of those wounds was to hold a small event commemorating the captures in the summer of 1997. Nichols Brothers Boat Builders of Freeland, Whidbey Island, provided transport for a boat trip to Penn Cove to honor the many whales stolen from their families.

In a concerted effort to pursue the growing Lolita campaign from the ground, in 1997, Garrett moved to Miami. For the next two years, he lived a hand-to-mouth existence in a cramped studio apartment, some might say akin to Lolita's life in her tiny tank. Numerous children's drawings, orca posters and collages of Lolita and her family decorated the walls. A poem titled "Imprisoned Too Long" adorned one wall; a couple of large cardboard boxes served as a makeshift filing cabinet; a laptop computer rested on a plywood desk. "My home is a Spartan apartment. NO TV." Garrett wrote in a Christmas newsletter. "But the Franklin Hotel two blocks away has dollar draft beer at happy hour, and I can run the remote sometimes."

Lolita Come Home!

Community Meeting
Thursday, Sept. 25
7 p.m.

Island County Courthouse
Commissioners Hearing Room
Sponsored by the Tokitae Foundation

Howard Garrett of the Tokitae Foundation & PAWS
will discuss the Lolita Come Home Project
& plans to bring the campaign to Miami

Come & learn how YOU can help
bring Lolita back home to Puget Sound

For more information call: **678-3451 or (360) 378-8654**

Left: Lolita Come Home; *Below*: Howard Garrett visits Lolita (1998). *Orca Network.*

For the first six months, Garrett lived on a $2,000 monthly stipend from PAWS. The nonprofit organization sponsored him to coordinate the Lolita project and spread the word to people in South Florida, including Hertz. When that money ran out, Garrett survived on occasional donations, bumper sticker and T-shirt sales, plus fundraisers and the goodwill of a few local businesses who helped out with printing costs. He walked the streets of Hollywood's Young Circle handing out flyers to shopkeepers, hanging thousands of "Free Lolita" posters and organizing a number of rallies outside the Seaquarium. A strong believer in the power of education (his book, *Orcas in Our Midst*, for middle-school children was published that year), Garrett visited numerous schools in Miami-Dade County, freelanced for various publications and met with the Honorable Alexander Penelas, mayor of Miami-Dade County, to explain orca cultures and why Lolita should be freed. Former Washington State attorney general Senator Slade Gorton (R), who represented the state in the 1976 lawsuit against SeaWorld, also wrote to Penelas supporting Lolita's return. In an effort to reach more people, Garrett designed his own website, which Microsoft representatives later redesigned free of charge.

Garrett's wife, Susan, (the couple married on June 18, 2005), one of four daughters born to Carmen and Oreste (Rusty) Berta, was brought up in Wyoming. She holds a bachelor of arts degree from Evergreen State College, Olympia, and moved to Whidbey Island in 1983. She first saw, and fell in love with, orcas on a whale-watching trip to Alaska. After dreaming about whales and telling the ship's captain next morning that they would spot them that day, her forecast came true. Orcas appeared and swam alongside the boat through a narrow passage at slack tide, a breathtaking experience that will remain indelibly imprinted on her memory forever.

While Garrett eked out a meager existence in Miami, Berta worked to raise funds to help support him from her base on Whidbey Island, where she worked as program coordinator of Island County Beach Watchers, a Washington State University extension program. It was through a slide presentation given to Beach Watchers by Wallie Funk (1922–2017), former co-owner of the *Anacortes American*, *Whidbey News-Times* and *South Whidbey Record* and the only professional journalist allowed to film the 1970 Penn Cove capture, that Berta first learned about Lolita. Funk told her there would be some people in attendance talking about a whale. Garrett introduced himself and told the group that there was still one whale alive out of those captured. He regaled them Lolita's story and spoke about the Free Lolita campaign. Berta immediately knew that she wanted to help in any way she

SLADE GORTON
WASHINGTON

APPROPRIATIONS

BUDGET

ENERGY AND NATURAL
RESOURCES

INDIAN AFFAIRS

United States Senate

WASHINGTON, DC 20510-4701

October 20, 1998

The Honorable Alex Penelas
Executive Mayor, Miami-Dade County
Stephen P. Clark Center
111 Northwest First Street, Suite 2910
Miami, Florida 33128-1994

Dear Mayor Penelas:

As the senior Senator from the state of Washington, I am writing to you today to request your assistance in returning the whale Lolita to her home waters off the coast of Washington. This issue was first addressed in our state back in 1995 with the formation of an organization designed to free Lolita. Since then this organization has grown stronger and larger but their purpose has remained the same: free Lolita and return her to her home in Puget Sound.

One of the key issues that I have been involved with this year in Washington D.C. is the restoration of our salmon runs. The citizens of our state believe in environmental stewardship and restoration. That is why I have worked so hard to try and find ways to bring back the salmon stocks. Returning Lolita to her natural habitat is yet another way to restore our ecosystem.

While I realize that Lolita is a major part of the Miami Seaquarium, I'm sure you can understand the desire of Washington state residents to see Lolita returned home. Thank you for your time and understanding.

Sincerely,

SLADE GORTON
United States Senator

SG ztl

"I am writing to request your assistance in returning the whale Lolita to her home waters." Letter Slade Gorton to Mayor Penelas, October 20, 1998. *Orca Network*

could. She became involved in the campaign and was invited to join the Tokitae Foundation board.

Despite Garrett's dedication and persistence, Lolita remained a prisoner. Not only was he fighting a shortage of funds and public apathy but also a powerful corporation. The Miami Seaquarium was the mainstay of the tourist economy in South Florida, with the owners supporting a number

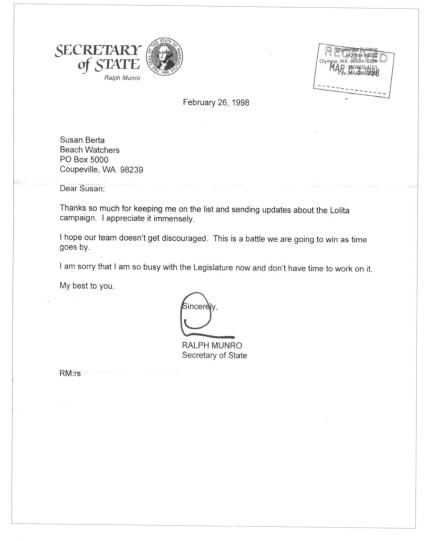

Susan Berta
Beach Watchers
PO Box 5000
Coupeville, WA 98239

Dear Susan:

Thanks so much for keeping me on the list and sending updates about the Lolita campaign. I appreciate it immensely.

I hope our team doesn't get discouraged. This is a battle we are going to win as time goes by.

I am sorry that I am so busy with the Legislature now and don't have time to work on it.

My best to you.

Sincerely,

RALPH MUNRO
Secretary of State

RM:rs

"This is a battle we are going to win as time goes by." Letter from Ralph Munro to Susan Berta, February 26, 1998. *Orca Network.*

of leading organizations, including the American Red Cross and Marine Mammal Stranding Network.

Realizing that a change of tactics might be needed, Garrett joined folk singer Jimmy Buffett's fan club, the Barefoot Children of Fort Lauderdale. He social-networked at the monthly meetings, distributing material about Lolita's cause, and talked to anyone who showed a flicker of interest. His efforts to discuss Lolita's future with Hertz were spurned. Hertz, who at the time drove a white Cadillac and owned a home in prestigious Coral Gables—plus a condo on exclusive Brickell Key, a man-made island off the mainland Brickell neighborhood of Miami—made it clear that the subject was not even up for discussion. He said of Garrett, "I think he should get a job. The man is doing something because he visualizes an awful lot of money and fame."

His unflattering comments did not end there. He claimed that Garrett lived in the Bahamas with Balcomb (Garrett vacationed there for two weeks with Balcomb, who was engaged in a long-term marine mammal research project) and accused him of making the occasional trip back to Miami to make it appear he was there full-time. He informed columnist David Letterman from the *Daily Business Review* that the half brothers ran a whale-watching organization in a cove in Puget Sound where they planned to take Lolita and that they would profit from her presence. That so-called whale-watching business is the nonprofit Center for Whale Research.

While fully supporting his younger brother's efforts, Balcomb cautioned, "I don't want to be pessimistic, but in my view Arthur is never going to talk about letting go of the whale." Garrett accepted that Balcomb was probably right but added, "I don't think he'll have any other choice."

Not only did Hertz refuse to discuss Lolita's future with Garrett, but on one occasion, together with three security officers, he also physically seized Garrett when he was at the Seaquarium as a guest of the chamber of commerce. Bobette Rousseau, a member of the chamber, witnessed Garrett being "escorted" from the premises and penned an indignant letter/facsimile about his treatment to the *Islander News*, Miami. Garrett fell afoul of the law in April 1998, when, on joining other protestors outside SeaWorld, Orlando, a photographer purportedly from *Orlando Sentinel* enticed the group to return to the entrance of SeaWorld, whereupon twelve police cars and a paddy wagon descended upon the scene and arrested the protestors for unlawful assembly.

Garrett was nothing if not tenacious. In spite of the daunting opposition, he continued to fight for Lolita's freedom, authoring and distributing a thirty-two-page report on the Lolita issue to local TV stations. He held a press conference and, with Powers's help, drew three hundred people to a fundraiser at South Beach's stylish Albion Hotel, raising $250. A number of influential people added their names to a sign-up sheet supporting Lolita's cause, but it later mysteriously disappeared. Fortunately, the donations they had contributed did not.

One big name who showed interest in supporting the Lolita campaign was British singer-songwriter/pianist Sir Elton John. Born Reginald Kenneth Dwight on March 25, 1947, he later changed his name to Elton Hercules John and was knighted by Queen Elizabeth II in 1998 for services to pop music and charity. In a signed letter dated May 4, 1999, sent to Garrett from John's London address, he wrote, "I have been deeply moved by the efforts to free Lolita, and wish to add my name to the campaign." When Garrett followed up with a call a week later, the musician's manager reneged, saying that they no longer wanted to play any part in the campaign.

While there was still no sign of a new tank, the *Miami Herald* reported that the Seaquarium had attempted to push legislation by seeking to add an amendment to an existing bill, rather than trying to introduce a separate

ELTON JOHN MANAGEMENT
7 KING ST CLOISTERS
CLIFTON WALK
W6 OGY
TEL: 0181 748 4800
FAX: 0181 741 7120

To whom it may concern:

I have been deeply moved by the efforts to free Lolita, and wish to add my name to the campaign to return her to home waters, where she can hopefully reunite with her family.

She has spent most of her life performing twice daily in a small tank, and I wish to add my voice to those others who are attempting to see her either freed, or fully cared for in retirement in a sea-pen within the waters where she was captured almost 30 years ago.

Signed ....
Sir Elton John

Date ....4th May 1999..........

"To whom it may concern." Letter from Sir Elton John, May 4, 1999. *Orca Network*.

bill that would exempt the Seaquarium from the county's Comprehensive Plan and let it begin a $70 million expansion—a project two courts, urged by residents from the nearby village of Key Biscayne, rejected. The village successfully blocked the expansion, fearing it would create traffic burdens along the Rickenbacker Causeway, the only access to and from the island. Hertz stated that the Seaquarium required renovation to bring it up to present-day standards, including a new tank for Lolita. The proposed expansion was expected to boost yearly attendance from 700,000 to more than a million. The refusal was a huge blow to the Seaquarium in its almost nine-year-long struggle to start construction of the Seaquarium Village.[27]

It was not the first time the Miami Seaquarium had run up against opposition. In 1991, the Metro-Dade County Commission approved a series of variances and expansions to demolish and redevelop the park. The decision was overturned by the Third District Court of Appeals as not permissible under the county's Comprehensive Plan, a decision upheld by the Florida Supreme Court. The County Commission amended the plan in 1994 to create an exemption for the Seaquarium. The Third District Court of Appeals overturned the commission's decision yet again, and in 1997, the governor and cabinet (acting as the Florida Administration Commission) directed Dade County not to amend the Comprehensive Plan for the Seaquarium, hence the attempt to seek a legislative exemption. Any faint glimmer of hope that there might be some improvement in Lolita's conditions was, once again, quashed.[28]

Although not wishing to be involved in the ongoing controversy surrounding Lolita, in September 1998, another huge corporation, Kodak (main corporate sponsor advertising "Kodak presents the Killer Whale Show") requested the Miami Seaquarium to remove the Kodak logo from the whale stadium and transferred its sponsorship to the Seaquarium's manatee program instead.

While Garrett continued fighting for Lolita's freedom in Miami, the plight of another captive orca, Corky II, came to the fore. Corky I, a female member of the A5 Northern Residents that frequent the coast of British Columbia, was captured in Pender Harbor, British Columbia, in April 1968; she died in December 1970 at Marineland of the Pacific, California. Corky II, another member of the A5 pod, was captured in Pender Harbor in December 1969; she, too, was sold to Marineland of the Pacific. When the park was taken over by SeaWorld in 1987 and subsequently closed, Corky II was transferred to SeaWorld, San Diego. She, like Lolita, has survived far beyond expectations, and is the longest-living orca in captivity.

"Sponsored by Kodak." View showing an animal trainer performing with an orca whale at the Miami Seaquarium attraction, no date. Color slide. *State Archives of Florida, Florida Memory Archives.*

Dr. Paul Spong, a well-known whale advocate based at OrcaLab, Hanson Island, British Columbia, spearheaded the Corky campaign. The Corky Freedom Bus, previously a Stuart Island (one of the San Juan Islands) school bus, was given a coat of fresh paint with Corky's profile emblazoned on one side and Lolita's profile on the other. The colorful creation set off from the Center for Whale Research with inveterate whale freedom fighter driver David Howitt at the wheel. Howitt, originally from Cornwall, England, drove to San Diego International Airport to collect the "Free Corky" banner after its return from Europe. Children from across the world had written "Free Corky" in many different languages on seventeen thousand patches of cloth, attached to a line by clothespins. Howitt then drove to San Francisco and up the West Coast, speaking to students about captivity. The tour heightened awareness of the plight of Corky, Lolita and the two orca clans to which they belonged, ending its journey at the Penn Cove Water Festival on Whidbey Island, close to the site of Lolita's capture.

Although at that time she was not such a high-profile whale as Keiko, who in September 1998 was moved to Iceland into a much larger ocean pen in preparation for training for his release, Lolita was becoming much better known. The twenty-eighth anniversary of the 1970 Penn Cove capture

Corky Freedom Bus. *Orca Network.*

Corky Freedom Banner. *Orca Network.*

took place in August with a sail to the capture site aboard Captain John Stone's ketch *Cutty Sark.* Stone, whose parents ran the Captain Whidbey Inn in Coupeville, ferried Funk out to photograph the capture scene. A number of political leaders attended the emotional event, as did John Crowe (1937–2015), one of the divers who had assisted in slitting open the bellies of the four dead calves before weighing them down with rocks in an attempt to hide the deaths. Q13 Fox News helped to spread Lolita's story to viewers in the Seattle area, and she gained international fame when TV channels across the UK broadcast *Lolita: Spirit in the Water.* Microsoft, one of the biggest corporations in the United States, posted a live message about her on a mega-traffic website that attracted an average sixty-five thousand daily visitors. The campaign was now gathering considerable momentum, its tentacles spreading across the globe. Lolita was no longer simply a box office attraction in Miami but a whale whose heart-wrenching story was permeating the hearts and minds of people around the world.

5
LOLITA'S DAY

I just sat and cried through the whole thing, using every bit of will power in my body and mind to keep from standing up and shouting to the people watching the show and clapping and cheering, 'Don't you know what you're watching?'" Berta wrote in a letter to the the *Coupeville Examiner* following her visit to the Miami Seaquarium on October 25, 1998.

Lolita performs the same twenty-minute mixture of tricks twice daily, early and late afternoon, seven days a week, fifty-two weeks a year. Extra shows are sometimes added. Up until June 2015, trainers rode on her back and rocket-hopped from her rostrum. After OSHA fined the Seaquarium for allowing trainers to work with Lolita without the right protection, the performers were no longer able to do water work with her.[29]

Visitors to the Seaquarium are asked to be at the Whale Bowl fifteen minutes before the show. As the gates open, eager tourists enter the stadium carrying GoPro cameras, soft drinks and trays of fast food. The static babble of conversation and high-pitched children's voices echo around the bleachers. Soon, loud, jarring rock music reverberates around the stands as people take their seats. Lolita's silhouette lies submerged in the center of the tank until she slowly breaks the surface and comes to rest in front of the feeding station, lifting her head slightly now and then. Unbeknownst to the spectators, this head lifting is known as a stereotypical behavior (abnormal repetitive behavior) seen in captive whales and dolphins. In the same way as a bear, tiger or elephant in a zoo might pace, captive cetaceans swim around and around the tank in circles, typically surfacing at the same spot.

Lolita waits to perform in the Whale Bowl. *Ingrid N. Visser, Orca Research Trust.*

Lolita's companions, Pacific white-sided dolphins, dart by. Constantly harassed by them, she pursues her tormentors briefly before sliding toward the corner of the tank, where wetsuited trainers shelter under a white umbrella from the intense heat of the Miami sun—but there is no shade for Lolita. As the relentless glare beats down on her back and dorsal fin, painted with zinc oxide to help protect her from the sun's unforgiving rays, the trainers chat with one another. The anthemic music steadily increases in volume as more people pour into the stadium. Lolita logs (rests at the surface) listlessly near the trainers, who ignore her. The waiting spectators, cellphones and selfie sticks in hand, chatter and laugh in anticipation of "a good show."

"For six to eight rows of the stadium you're in a great spot to see the show—you're also in a great spot to get wet with very cold splashing salt water," the announcer warns the audience, adding that this is the only chance they'll have to move if they don't want to get soaked; the same words are repeated in Spanish for the benefit of the many Hispanic visitors who make up a large part of the Seaquarium's revenue. Lolita continues to log near the trainers' station. Cameras are constantly clicking.

The dolphins speed around the tank as Lolita waits for her moment. A trainer parades around the outside of the perimeter fence in front of the

No shelter for Lolita from the hot Miami sun. *Ingrid N. Visser, Orca Research Trust.*

audience, vigorously waving and clapping. After a brief introduction about the Seaquarium, the rest of the trainers are introduced. More arm waving follows in time with the discordant music, then, right on cue, Lolita breaches. Stunt over, she swims to the food station, where she is offered a reward of dead fish. Once again on cue, she turns over onto her back, waving her pectoral fins as the spectators applaud and cheer.

A slight lull in the ear-splitting rock medley allows the trainer to speak about killer whales living in all the oceans of the world. Reference is made to the three pods of the endangered Southern Resident population, describing Lolita as special, an ambassador for her kind, enabling people to connect with this beautiful endangered species—but no one says how she came to be there or that the capture era is one of the reasons the Southern Resident population is listed under the ESA.

After Lolita circles the tank, slapping the water with her tail flukes, she returns to the feeding station and makes a siren sound. A child shrieks in delight at the spectacle of a killer whale vocalizing—or so the child believes. It is not a vocalization (whales make noise by squeezing air between balloon-like sacs in their heads), which is how orcas communicate, but "burping" through the blowhole. After sporting her flukes, Lolita opens her jaws wide and begs for more fish.

"A big, wet splash" from Lolita. *Howard Garrett.*

Ocean Sun (L25) breaches in the Salish Sea. *Carrie Sapp.*

Lolita begs for food. *Ingrid N. Visser, Orca Research Trust.*

Ocean Sun (L25) takes a look around. *David Ellifrit, Center for Whale Research.*

The show draws to a close. In preparation for the grand finale, the trainers pose on the concrete barrier between the main pool and the medical pool, waving their arms to whip up the audience one more time. Lolita cartwheels, splashing cold, chlorinated water over the side of the perimeter fence and onto the screaming crowd.

Summoning her reserves of energy, Lolita propels herself upward into a back flip, thrashing her flukes back and forth and dousing the tourists one more time. With a last wave of her pectoral fins, she returns to the food station for her reward and enrichment time. She is given her favorite toy, an old wetsuit. (She and Hugo effectively removed a wetsuit from a trainer in 1975.) A plastic ball, boat fenders and a thin trickle of water from a narrow hose are the other toys that make up playtime for Lolita. After taking a few more photographs, the audience dribbles out of the stadium. Show over, the trainers return to their tasks, ignoring Lolita. After they, too, leave and the gates are locked for the night, Lolita returns to her life of solitude, alone but for the Pacific white-sided dolphins and their unwelcome attention. They, like Lolita, have nowhere to go, their lives no more fulfilled than that of Lolita. Seeking distractions from their boredom, Lolita is an easy target.

As darkness falls, jet planes bringing in fresh intakes of tourists fly over the Seaquarium, unwittingly witnessing Lolita's misery. Perhaps tomorrow they will wait in line to buy a ticket for the killer whale show, one more item to cross off the bucket list.

At night, people at the adjacent University of Miami's Rosenstiel School of Marine and Atmospheric Science campus hear Lolita repeatedly vocalizing the S-1, S-22 and S-40 calls she learned from her mother many years ago. But there is no answer; her family members are far, far away. Such is the reality of life for Lolita.

6

THE WHALE BOWL

On May 9, 1999, the first of many symbolic Mother's Day demonstrations took place in front of the Miami Seaquarium. Mother's Day, which goes back in history to the ancient Greeks and Romans, is a celebration of honoring one's mother and the influence of mothers in society. Orcas are a matriarchal society, and as Lolita's probable mother is still alive, it was a fitting tribute. Proof positive of the relationship has never been obtained, as although DNA samples have been taken of Ocean Sun and Lolita by Dr. Michael J. Ford, Northwest Fisheries Science Center, Seattle, and Professor A. Rus Hoelzel of Durham University, United Kingdom, respectively, Hoelzel has not released the results of his research despite a request to do so.

Ocean Sun, estimated to have been born in 1928, was named in 1983 as the result of a contest held in Victoria, British Columbia, to name all members of L pod as part of a campaign to prevent the issuing of a Canadian permit to capture more orcas for public display. Her daughter Tsunami (L23) died in 1982 at an estimated age of thirty; Tsunami's probable offspring Cordy (L44) died in 1989 at around age seventeen, and Tsunami's only other known calf, L49 (unnamed), died in 1980 after one year.

With no immediate family of her own, for many years, Ocean Sun traveled with then matriarch of the Southern Resident community, Granny (J2). The much-loved orca, estimated to have been born in 1911, was declared missing at the close of 2016. With the loss of Granny, Ocean Sun is now the matriarch of the Southern Resident community; she often travels with Mega (L41) and his sisters Matia (L77) and Calypso (L94).

Ocean Sun (L25) in her natal waters. *David Ellifrit, Center for Whale Research.*

Two people who had supported orca freedom for many years, Ralph Munro and his wife, attended the demonstration with their son, George. It was the first time in her life that Karen Munro had taken part in a public demonstration.

With around fifteen police cars surrounding the park, 150 to 200 people from California, Missouri, Virginia and Washington peacefully marched in front of the Seaquarium entrance, holding flags, signs and banners asking for Lolita's release. Passing cars honked in support. Lolita's family calls were played, amplified by a bullhorn. Fearful of disruption, the Seaquarium canceled her first performance, declaring how unethical and inhumane it would be to release her. Berta described the demonstration, which was covered by three Miami TV stations: "I arrived in Miami the morning of the event….Though this event took place in Miami, there were hundreds of folks in Washington who were here in heart and spirit, and I came bearing best wishes and thoughts from Toki's extended human 'family' back home."

Berta revealed that, earlier in the week orcas were seen in Penn Cove not just once, but twice, an extremely rare occurrence since the fateful 1970 and 1971 captures.

Former dolphin trainer and Miami Seaquarium employee Laura Singer, who was also present, said, "I think everyone that worked with her [Lolita]

579-6440

Application
Feb 18 '99

THE CITY OF MIAMI
POLICE

Department of Police
City of Miami

Off Duty Employment
Application Form

APPLICATION FOR DEMONSTRATION

NAME OF REQUESTING ORGANIZATION: *Tokitae Foundation*

PERSON REQUESTING PERMIT: *Howard Garrett*

ON SCENE PERSON RESPONSIBLE FOR DEMONSTRATION: *Howard Garrett*

DEMONSTRATION SITE: *Public land along road - in front of Miami Seaquarium*

DATE OF OCCURRENCE: *May 9, 1999* START TIME: *12 noon*

END TIME: *2 pm* NUMBER OF PARTICIPANTS: *100 - 250*

PURPOSE OF DEMONSTRATION: *To express opinion that Lolita, the orca on display, be returned to native water*

OFFICER/UNIT MONITORING DEMONSTRATION: _____

ADDRESS OF ORGANIZATION: *920 Meridian Ave #2 Miami Beach 33139* PHONE: *672-4039*

ADDRESS OF PERSON REQUESTING: *same* PHONE (WORK): *same*

PHONE (HOME): *same*

IDENTIFICATION PRESENTED: *Florida driver's licence*

SIGNATURE OF APPLICANT: *Howard Garrett*

UNITS NOTIFIED: COPY OF IDENTIFICATION:

FSS MAJOR: YES NO

DISTRICT MAJOR: YES NO
NAME:_____
NET LIEUTENANT: YES NO
NAME:_____
SIS: YES NO
NAME:_____

Application to demonstrate outside Miami Seaquarium on Mother's Day, May 9, 1999. *Orca Network.*

would vote for her retirement if it didn't mean losing their job. She has jumped enough and splashed enough. Too bad we can't find an attorney to take on her case." Singer admitted that she had been unaware that Lolita's family was still in Puget Sound. She spoke of her time at the Seaquarium and how she had provided Lolita with the companionship and kindness that was not always forthcoming from the male trainers.

Howard Garrett rallies the crowd. *Orca Network.*

Garrett and Berta appealing for Lolita's freedom. *Orca Network.*

Flipper, the dolphin star, rests next to aquamaid Laura Singer at the Miami Seaquarium, 1973. Black & white photoprint, 3 x 4 in. *State Archives of Florida, Florida Memory.*

Singer also supplied documentation dating back to 1970 showing that the Seaquarium knew all along that orcas use complex language and live in tightly bonded societies. Four pages of sound bites had been written about killer whales for the Seaquarium by Jane Wallace, an investigative reporter for the now-defunct *Miami News* and the mother of the late Janet Reno (attorney general to President Clinton and the first woman to serve as attorney general, from 1993 to 2001). The sound bites specifically stated that "the killer whale is highly social. Family togetherness is a way of life," and "their language seems to be quite complex." The longevity of orcas' lives was also known by referral to Australia's "Old Tom," who lived to at least eighty years of age.

The documentation revealed that the depth of the medical pool was only ten feet deep—not twelve feet deep. According to the architects' drawings, the depth of the main pool was only eighteen feet deep—not twenty feet deep. Garrett states that, at some point, the Seaquarium added two feet (in the documentation) to the water level. More relevant to the legal status of the tank, however, was the medical pool, which was counted in the overall dimensions by APHIS.

Lolita's tank is, and has been, the subject of contention for many years. As far back as 1978, Lolita's then trainer Michael Royce traveled to Washington, D.C., to testify before the USDA that the tank housing Hugo and Lolita was inadequate. The USDA advised Royce that, although the tank was too small, the Seaquarium had informed them that they would soon be building a new one.

Reportedly measuring seventy-three feet wide and eighty feet long, the Whale Bowl doubles as a performance pool and holding area. It is the smallest and oldest orca tank in the United States, considered by many to be illegal by government standards and in violation of the Animal Welfare Act (AWA). This act, passed by Congress in 1966, was introduced to regulate the treatment of animals in research and display. Despite the incorporation of various amendments, the last being in 2013, it remains woefully inadequate as far as the welfare of captive marine mammals is concerned.

Both the AWA and APHIS, the agency responsible for administering the AWA, state that the main enclosure should be forty-eight feet wide in either direction with a straight line of travel across the middle. Lolita's tank is only thirty-five feet from the front wall to the slide-out barrier and, at its deepest central point, twenty feet deep—Lolita is approximately twenty feet long. (Southern Resident females grow to between seventeen and twenty-one feet). The AWA allows an orca to be kept in a tank *only* twelve feet deep. A further requirement is that perimeter fences "less than six feet high for other marine mammals must be approved in writing by the Administrator." Lolita's tank does not have a six-foot perimeter fence around it. Was the fence approved by an administrator? There is no protection for Lolita from direct sunlight or from the weather—including hurricanes—that batter the Florida coastline.

Despite a complaint by the Humane Society of the United States (HSUS) in 1995 claiming that the then twenty-five-year-old tank failed to meet AWA minimum size regulations in accordance with AWA 9. CFR. Section. 3.104 (Space Requirements), APHIS has repeatedly renewed the Seaquarium's license. Why?

To be compliant with the AWA, the minimum space requirements need four factors to be satisfied for tanks holding cetaceans like Lolita. These are depth, volume, surface area and minimum horizontal dimension (MHD) of forty-eight feet. Inspectors concluded that although the first three requirements were met, the concrete island at the center of Lolita's tank made it non-compliant for MHD unless this was waived. However, in 1999, inspectors approved the tank and said no waiver was needed as "while there is a platform in this pool that does intersect with the required minimum horizontal dimension, there is nothing in the regulations that prohibits such an object from being in the pool."[30]

Section 3.128 of the AWA space requirements state that the width of an enclosure for a dolphin or orca must be at least twice the length of the animal. Regulators add the dimensions of the medical pool to the main pool to arrive at a legal measurement.

Garrett contacted the USDA and requested that further measurements of both the tank and depth of the medical pool be taken. He also asked for an explanation as to why the architects' drawings and the USDA measurements were different. The USDA stated that the department had used an independent engineer to take the measurements but refused to provide a name without a Freedom of Information Act (FOIA) request. In response to a further request for the engineer's name, the USDA replied that, due to a backlog of requests, it would not be possible to find the name "for months."

As stated by HSUS:

> *Clearly, whatever the principal reason for their ranging patterns, confining cetaceans in a pool that is at best only six or seven times their body length guarantees a lack of aerobic conditioning and brings on the endless stereotypical behaviors seen in other large carnivores in captivity. Such confinement is inhumane at a nearly inconceivable level.*

Dr. Naomi Rose added, "The Seaquarium is in clear violation of the regulations and APHIS has been aware of this ongoing violation yet has done nothing to correct it."

Although APHIS served notice in the *Federal Register* of proposed rule changes concerning the minimum space requirements for captive marine mammals in 2002, saying that it had discretion to change the space requirements for orcas in captivity and, if petitioned to do so, would "respond accordingly," nothing came of it; the agency later maintained that no noncompliant items were found.

As Garrett described in an interview with *National Enquirer*, "Lolita suffers loneliness and isolation twenty-four hours a day.…It's exactly like locking a person into a six-by-eight-foot cell for life and never again allowing him to see another human being."[31] Following Garrett's interview, *National Enquirer* wrote to Senator Bob Graham (D), former governor of Florida, saying,

Lolita stands on her tail in the eighteen-feet-deep section and slowly bobs up and down with at least four feet of her head and upper body out of the water....Both Lolita and the four dolphins that share the pool keep their eyes squinted nearly shut because THERE IS NO SHADE ANYWHERE.

The published article included a coupon to send to the senator stating, "I am outraged that Lolita the orca has been kept in a tiny tank in the Miami Seaquarium for 29 years. Please contact the USDA administrator Ron DeHaven and insist upon Lolita's release to the wild." The paper, which claimed to have sixteen million readers, announced that it had received fourteen thousand letters and would be running another story. Hertz, true to form, turned down the tabloid's request for an interview.

Just as they had done before, children rallied to support Lolita's cause. Students from G.W. Carver Middle School in Coral Gables, a public school for international education and studies, distributed a petition calling on Senator Graham to intercede on Lolita's behalf by filing a complaint with the USDA to enforce the AWA.

A further violation of the AWA relates to Section 3.109, which states that "marine mammals, whenever known to be primarily social in the wild, must be housed in their primary enclosure with at least one compatible animal of the same or biologically related species." The Southern Residents are a social structure of orcas consisting of generations of family. There is no known case of a Southern Resident leaving the pod to live with Pacific white-sided dolphins. As Garrett pointed out,

Probably the least understood aspect of orcas that may also be the most important for understanding their social behavior, their bonds, their unique vocalizations and their highly coordinated group behavior is that they live every minute of their lives according to traditions learned from birth as members of ancient cultures.

Two weeks after the Mother's Day demonstration, Berta visited Lolita again. When she had finished touring the park, which she described as "small and dismal," Berta said,

I walked up to the edge of Toki's tank hoping to get to spend some quality time with her before the awful antics of show biz began. She was over at the trainers' island with her back to me, but as soon as I reached the edge of the pool she immediately turned around and made a beeline toward me.

"Coming 2002." Future site of new whale and dolphin stadium at the Miami Seaquarium. *Orca Network*

She came right up to me and stayed there most of the twenty minutes with her nose right up to my face.

Unlike Berta's previous visit, when Lolita spent most of the time motionless at the bottom of the tank (Visser has observed that of all the whales she has studied, Lolita and Corky, both wild-caught, exhibit this behavior in captivity), Lolita stayed close by moving her head from side to side, sometimes opening her mouth, at other times swimming sideways around the tank's perimeter watching Berta and only occasionally going to the bottom of the tank. Berta was encouraged to see Lolita in a more sociable mood. In as far as it could be, it was a rewarding encounter.

Whether the public demonstration provoked Hertz to speak out publicly or not is a matter of conjecture. For the first time in four years, he appeared on Miami's Channel 10 News and announced that, although the Seaquarium had given up on attempts to gain exemption from the zoning regulations for a planned $70 million expansion, he would still build a new 2.2 million–gallon tank for Lolita with construction due to start in six months. He also said he intended to find a mate for her so that the pair could breed. No one could have anticipated just how unscrupulous Wometco Enterprises would prove in an attempt to find that mate.

7

KEIKO, LUNA AND SPRINGER

In July 1999, the dark side of captivity reared its ugly head once more when Tilikum, who was now at SeaWorld, Orlando, claimed the life of Daniel Dukes. Dukes, who had likely entered the park undetected at night, was discovered draped over Tilikum's back the next morning. Notwithstanding the speculation regarding the circumstances surrounding Dukes's death, it was a sharp reminder of the latent aggression lying dormant in captive killer whales.

While the August commemoration of Lolita's capture took place on Whidbey Island, Garrett presented the Seaquarium with a further proposal to allow Lolita to communicate with her family. Following a demonstration outside the Seaquarium, the BBC program *Up All Night* requested a telephone interview with Garrett to discuss the "Lolita Phone Home" proposal, which was subsequently broadcast in the UK. Morning newsstands and business offices receiving the *Miami Daily Business Review* were treated to this headline: "Lolita—Call Your Mom!"

Following his two-year stint in Miami kick-starting the Lolita campaign, in November 1999, Garrett returned to Whidbey Island. He and Berta worked on raising awareness about the environmental issues surrounding the population decline of the Southern Residents and the interconnectedness between orcas, salmon and ecosystems. Their mission included the implementation of a volunteer network to track whales in and around Island County, Washington State, promoting shore-based whale watching and educational outreach. The Tokitae Foundation launched the Orcas in Our

"Lolita, Call Your Mom." *Orca Network*.

Midst Educational Outreach Program by publishing volume 2 of Garrett's middle school booklet *Orcas in Our Midst*.

A new edition of the award-winning documentary *Orcas in the Balance*, originally made in 1998 by Overport Productions and People for Puget Sound, was also produced. A poster display for classrooms and an activity guide to accompany speaking engagements were distributed to business and government entities throughout western Washington. The power of education was considered the key to reaching a wide cross-section of the public.

Despite having told the press that there would be no more attempts to expand the Seaquarium, in December 1999, Garrett was advised by a Florida state representative that the Seaquarium did, in fact, try to convince the legislature once again to allow the park to override county zoning regulations and build a $70 million nightclub and restaurant on the site owned by Miami-Dade County. County regulations state that the property must be used for a "marine recreational area," which clearly rules out a nightclub. And not surprisingly, six months after Hertz announced his intention to build a new tank for Lolita, there was still no sign of one.

The Seaquarium's water supply, in which all the marine mammals swim and live, is drawn from Biscayne Bay. In June 2000, Lolita's life and that of the other animals at the Seaquarium was under threat when contractors working on a pier at Miami Beach Marina, without a proper permit, accidentally crushed an underwater pipe from Miami Beach to Virginia Key, spilling twenty to thirty-five million gallons of sewage into the bay. Fishing and bathing were banned at beaches to prevent outbreaks of salmonella poisoning or viral diarrhea. The ban lasted for almost ten days, with beaches reopening just in time for the Fourth of July.

Less than a year after the crushing of the underwater pipe, Lolita's survival was once again threatened after millions of gallons of raw sewage spilled into Biscayne Bay when a tugboat raked the bottom, splitting open a main sewer line. An eight-foot-wide fountain of waste spewed four feet above the surface of the water. It was estimated that between seven and twelve million gallons of sewage could have ended up in coastal waters, and beaches were once again closed to the public.[32]

Orcas in Our Midst by Howard Garrett. *Author collection.*

The year 2001 was not a good one for Lolita's family. The Center for Whale Research census, which is conducted in July, showed that seven orcas were missing, leaving only seventy-eight in the community—a marked decrease from ninety-eight in 1995. An MSNBC documentary on the Southern Residents' well-being highlighted the stress of depleted salmon runs, increased boat traffic and the effects of ingesting toxins such as polychlorinated biphenyls (PCBs)—used in transformers and other electrical equipment—and polybrominated diphenyl ethers (PBDEs)—flame retardants—as contributory factors to their decline. Although much of the story concerned boat/whale interactions, it made clear that the most effective way to ensure that orcas remained in the Salish Sea was to restore salmon, many runs of which were listed as endangered.

With increasing concerns surrounding the survival of the Southern Residents, in an attempt to safeguard their future, on May 1, 2001, a number of nonprofit organizations petitioned the government to list the Southern Residents under the ESA.[33] Under this act, distinct population segments (DPS) are afforded all the protections available. Being classified as both "discrete" and "significant," the Southern Residents qualified as a distinct population segment. The petition also advocated for "the release and reintroduction of captive whales taken from this population."

But while orca numbers were decreasing, awareness about their intelligence and abilities was increasing. A paper in the prestigious British journal of *Behavioural and Brain Sciences* titled "Culture in Whales and Dolphins," by Luke Rendell and Hal Whitehead, produced compelling evidence about the lives of orcas, revealing how each community, determined by cultural rules, has its own vocabulary and behavioral preferences, from food choices to mating partners. In the words of Rendell and Whitehead, "[T]he complex and stable vocal and behavioral cultures of sympatric (overlapping) groups of killer whales (*Orcinus orca*) appear to have no parallel outside humans, and represent an independent evolution of cultural faculties."[34]

Not long after conducting the 2001 census, the CFWR announced that Luna (L98), born in September 1999, was missing. The center's policy is to have at least three encounters with a pod before declaring a whale missing. Luna's mother, Splash (L67), belonged to Lolita's sub-pod. A month later, a single killer whale was spotted in Nootka Sound on the northwest coast of Vancouver Island, an area normally frequented by the Northern Residents. If this was the missing Southern Resident Luna, he was a long way from home. Believing the orca to be the reincarnation of the local Mowachaht/Muchalaht tribe's late chief, Ambrose Maquinna, who declared that after his death he wanted to return as an orca or wolf, Chief Mike Maquinna gave Luna a traditional native name, Tsu'xiit.

There had been questions over Luna's parentage since his birth. Garrett first saw the calf in September 1999 when Luna and his mother, Splash, swam past the Center for Whale Research. In Garrett's words, it was almost as if she was bringing Luna by to show him off. He was, after all, her first known calf. However, the rest of L pod was nowhere to be seen. Later that day, mother and son rejoined L pod, with K pod in the vicinity. The next time Luna was sighted, he was with Kiska (K18). This pattern continued until he was sighted once again with Splash prior to his disappearance.

Researchers speculated that Luna may have become separated from his pod when his uncle Orcan (L39) died, based on the theory that Orcan was sick and could not keep up with the pod. Luna may have stayed with him and during that time lost track of L pod. Adult males and their nephews often travel together, and Splash's record as a mother straying from her calf raised suspicions. Usually mothers and calves are tightly bonded, with the calf nursing for at least a year and swimming in the mother's slipstream, the area of least resistance.

In a twist of irony, while researchers endeavored to solve the mystery of the young orca seen near Vancouver Island, a new drama was evolving in Washington State with the arrival in January 2002 of an orphaned calf in Puget Sound. First seen in Swinomish Channel, La Conner, and identified as A73, a member of the Northern Resident population, the calf, born late 1999 or early 2000, was known as Springer. While she roamed Puget Sound, the missing Southern Resident orca now positively identified as Luna wandered Nootka Sound.

In Miami, the Animal Rights Foundation of Florida (ARFF) teamed up with the newly formed Orca Conservancy (formerly the Tokitae Foundation), soon to become Orca Network, to add its weight to the Free Lolita campaign. Together with Florida state representative Gus Barreiro (R), about sixty people demonstrated outside the Seaquarium on the thirty-first anniversary of Lolita's capture. Before the demonstration, Barreiro called Hertz to let him know he was initiating a high-profile public awareness drive to gain Lolita's freedom. Possibly prompted by the prospect of adverse publicity, the Seaquarium held a press briefing on August 2, 2001, reiterating that it would soon begin construction of a new tank for Lolita that would take eighteen to twenty-four months to complete.

By now, demonstrations outside the Seaquarium were a regular event on weekends. Two members of the ARFF, cinematographer Tim Gorski and film producer/ecologist Valerie Silidker, who co-founded Rattle the Cage Productions, decided to make their own mark on the Mother's Day protest when, similar to the January demonstration during which four protestors disrupted the show by displaying their Free Lolita T-shirts and informing the spectators why Lolita should be freed, they entered the stadium.[35] At

"We're building a whale of a home." Reader-board at Miami Seaquarium, 2001. *Orca Network.*

the quietest moment during the show, when the blaring rock-and-roll music is turned down and the audience told, "If everyone's really quiet, you'll be able to hear Lolita speak," the pair displayed their Free Lolita shirts and proceeded to educate the public about Lolita's capture, the illegal status of her tank and her ability to return home and rejoin her family. This was a far cry from the type of education the Seaquarium wanted people to hear. When asked later about the audience's reaction, Gorski replied that the majority of people booed. He recalls one woman shouting, "You're ruining my kids' show." After the security guards moved in to escort the couple from the stadium, according to Gorski, he was pushed down the stairs during the ensuing fracas, bruising and spraining his arm.[36]

Following a yearlong status review to determine whether the Southern Resident killer whales warranted listing under the ESA, on June 25, 2002, NMFS denied the petition on the grounds that the Southern Residents did not qualify for listing as they did not constitute a "species" as defined under the ESA. Bowing to the political stance at the time, under the Bush administration, the Southern Residents were not considered "significant," in essence, if they became extinct, another population would simply move in and replace them. NMFS stated that they would reassess the whales' status under the ESA within the next four years or if information came to light indicating that the whales were a "species" within the meaning of the ESA. The agency sought instead to list the Southern Residents as "depleted" under the MMPA. Dissatisfied with the ruling, Earthjustice Legal Defense Fund and the Center for Biological Diversity gave the agency a sixty-day notice of intent to sue over violations of Section 4 of the ESA.

While conflict and bureaucratic wrangling surrounded the Southern Residents, concerted efforts to reunite Springer with her pod continued. Six months after her unexpected arrival in Puget Sound, she was transported the four hundred miles to a sea-pen in Dong Chong Bay, near Johnstone Strait, British Columbia, by Catalina Jet, a type of catamaran supplied by Nichols Brothers Boat Builders, the same company that supplied the boat for the Penn Cove commemoration cruise.

David Howitt, who was sitting on rocks listening to hydrophones through headphones, was fortunate to witness Springer's reaction when her pod swam into the area. He spoke of hearing Springer's calls, which turned to screeches when her family was in range and she could hear their vocalizations. Her calls sounded desperate to Howitt, which he says he found distressing. However, this was one story that would have a happy ending. When Springer's calls returned to normal, Howitt could hear her communicating with her pod. The following day, she was released from the sea-pen and successfully reintegrated with her family, the Northern Residents. Since then, she has given birth to two calves. Like Lolita, her ancestry and locale were known, making the chances of acceptance by her family much more likely. It is impossible not to wonder how Lolita would react if she, too, were given the same chance as Springer.

Meanwhile, Luna remained alone in an increasingly precarious situation. Thousands of visitors flocked to Gold River to see the playful, sociable orca, who, like Springer, sought company by following boats, putting both himself and members of the public at risk. Concern for Luna's safety and that of the boating fraternity triggered a complex chain of personal and political agendas, the ramifications of which Luna would, alas, eventually fall victim.

After twenty years of captivity and three years of preparation for return to the wild, Keiko left his sea-pen in Iceland at the end of July. For those who had helped bring Keiko to this point, it was a highly emotional moment. Keiko was now in charge of his own destiny. But if the Seaquarium had its way, his freedom would be short-lived. Keen to find a mate for Lolita, within six weeks of Keiko's release, Wometco Enterprises wrote to NMFS on

Visitors flock to see Luna in Gold River, British Columbia. *Doreen Semmens.*

September 9, 2002, requesting a permit to rescue and import Keiko under NMFS's emergency regulations. It cited as grounds for the application that Keiko was not swimming with a pod, "which is an indication that he is being rejected by other orcas," and was seeking human companionship. The final paragraph of their letter read, "We would like to rescue Keiko and bring him to our facility in Miami, where he would receive the best of care and would be able to live out his remaining years in safety and in the company of Lolita, a docile and friendly female orca."

Two days later, on September 11, Wometco Enterprises wrote a similar letter to the Norwegian Directorate of Fisheries, offering to rescue Keiko and take him to Miami, where he would receive medical care and be able to live out his remaining years in safety alongside Lolita. So eager was the company to gain ownership of Keiko that, in addition to the letter to the Norwegian Directorate of Fisheries, it wrote to NMFS again that day. The second letter stated that, while the company understood that NMFS could not issue a permit to import Keiko until it had custody of the animal, the Seaquarium had completed all the information required for an import and display permit to assist NMFS in preparing the emergency permit.

Invitation to Discovery Channel premier of *Keiko, Born to Be Wild*, 1999. *Orca Network*.

Incensed by the Seaquarium's blatant attempt to deprive Keiko of his hard-earned freedom and still fighting to turn the tide of disbelief, Garrett wasted no time in contacting the media. He urged people to write to the Norwegian government objecting to the application, arguing that not only was the application for a permit to capture Keiko a violation of the whale's hard-won freedom but also that Lolita's tank was too small for one whale, let alone two.

Much to the Seaquarium's disappointment, the Norwegian government and NMFS blocked the attempt to recapture Keiko. They advised Wometco Enterprises that the application was premature and informed the company that the Norwegian government "is not considering allowing the capture of Keiko by the Miami Seaquarium or any other entity."

Bringing a year to a close in which both wild and captive whales received wide media coverage, on December 18, 2002, a coalition of environmental groups and individuals filed suit against NMFS, challenging the agency's decision not to declare the Southern Resident orcas as endangered. If the agency thought that classifying the Southern Residents as depleted under the MMPA was sufficient to satisfy those seeking greater protection for the orcas, it had badly miscalculated.

8

SLAVE TO ENTERTAINMENT

Far from acting as a deterrent, Gorski's unfortunate experience at the Miami Seaquarium was the spur for another movie about Lolita. In January 2003, the provocative documentary titled *Lolita: Slave to Entertainment*, produced by Gorski and narrated by Silidker, was released. Described as "the film that an entire industry would rather you not see," it portrays graphic imagery of Lolita's capture and includes interviews with some of those present at the time. As O'Barry commented, "When you capture a creature like Lolita and put her in this concrete box, you take away the two most important aspects of her life: her family and the world of sound." The film was a great success, winning Best Documentary Award at the New Jersey Film Festival and Best Feature Documentary Award at the Newport Beach Film Festival in California.

The production of the film and Gorski's complaint against the Seaquarium following the alleged assault in 2002 resulted in court action. Gorski claimed that because he refused to settle (which would mean forfeiting the film and website), the Seaquarium filed a counterclaim demanding over $300,000 in supposed damages and a complete cease and desist of the award-winning film. Wometco Enterprises alleged that Gorski disrupted the whale show by protesting for his animal rights' cause and arranging for the protest to be filmed. It also claimed that he trespassed and took additional film of Lolita and the Seaquarium, which he used in the movie, thus distributing, displaying and/or selling the film to third parties as part of his animal rights activities. Gorski countersued for harassment, and two years later, the suit was settled out of court for an undisclosed sum.

Following submission of taped evidence by Russ Rector, Dolphin Freedom Foundation, regarding violations at the Seaquarium, Miami-Dade County building officials carried out surprise inspections of the premises on September 11 and 12, 2003. The violations included, but were not limited to, crumbling concrete and loose, corroded guardrails on stairways and viewing decks (including the bridge over the shark moat). In the words of County Building Chief Charles Danger, there were "exposed wires everywhere, open electrical boxes everywhere, light posts where the wiring is bad everywhere."[37] Danger ordered that a tank used for the treatment of sick animals be cordoned off and the animals removed, as the supports holding up the roof were severely deteriorated. Some sections of the park were closed, and the Seaquarium was given the weekend to rectify matters or risk being shut down on Monday.

Inspectors also compiled a list of less urgent code violations, including repair work carried out on the manatee tank without the necessary permits. The Seaquarium was required to correct those matters within thirty days. With Lolita being the park's star attraction, rapid repairs were made to the stands surrounding her tank so that the show could go on.

Although Hertz denied that any of the violations were a threat to the public or to employees, Danger stated that he had found abundant evidence of long-neglected repairs. "You can see that they were patching here and patching there, and patching on patches, and they have been doing this for some time."

Many of the problems had gone unnoticed by the county for years, as inspections were usually carried out only when complaints arose or owners obtained permits to carry out work. Although structures older than forty years had to be inspected and recertified every ten years (many of the Seaquarium buildings were nearing fifty years of age), such inspections were conducted by private engineers hired by the owners, who then certified that the buildings met the required codes.

A month later, Dolphin Freedom Foundation hired an independent safety inspector, W. Jon Wallace, to investigate potential hazards at the Seaquarium. Wallace, in the capacity of a visitor, conducted a walk-through inspection on October 10 and 11, 2003. His overall assessment was that numerous significant safety concerns existed, in particular with regard to the Flipper Show, Golden Dome Sea Lion Show and the Killer Whale Show. Each of the assembly areas was equipped with only two exits; four exits were required to align with the National Fire Protection Association Life Safety Code. Wallace noted that several violations had been discovered by the Miami-Dade County Fire Marshal's Office during its recent inspection—these were never cited by that department during previous routine scheduled inspections.[38]

According to an article in the *Florida Sun-Sentinel*,[39] the Miami-Dade County Fire Marshal's Office planned to allow the violation to be abated by adding *one* additional exit (which meant the Seaquarium would not have to reduce seating capacity), resulting in a total of three exits rather than the four stipulated as per the National Environmental Policy Act (NEPA), a piece of legislation enacted on January 1, 1970. It is one of the shortest laws in existence, amounting to fewer than six pages. In order to comply with the statutory requirements, the whale stadium was closed for "enhancements" in November, reopening on December 21—just in time for Christmas.

While Lolita was having an unexpected break from performing, Canada's Department of Fisheries and Oceans (DFO) agreed that, although Luna should be taken back to his home territory, the department did not have the monetary resources to implement the proposal. However, when NMFS stepped up with funding, the Canadian government followed suit. Even so, Luna was not going anywhere yet. Although funding was now available, DFO decided it was too late in the year to proceed with any transfer. Luna's prospective move would remain in abeyance until the U.S. and Canadian governments could meet and agree to a fresh reunification plan. By now, the lively, sociable whale had a sister, Aurora (L101), as Splash gave birth to her second calf in September 2002.

During his two years of freedom, Keiko had traveled many miles and flirted with different orca pods, a lifestyle far removed from the constraints of a concrete tank. Sadly, on November 12, 2003, news broke that Keiko had died in Taknes Fjord, Norway, apparently from acute pneumonia. David Phillips, president and founder of the Free Willy–Keiko Foundation, stated, "Keiko was a trailblazer, the first orca whale ever rescued from captivity. Keiko showed what is possible if these animals are just given the chance."[40]

To this day, many people argue that Keiko was not a good candidate for release. His chances might have been better for longer term survival had Balcomb's advice to locate Keiko's pod been heeded. Orcas gather behind trawlers when nets are hauled in, so it would not have been too difficult to take blubber samples and match the DNA. Balcomb firmly believed that if Keiko was in the vicinity of his pod they would have recognized something about him, even though he was only around two years of age when captured. As he told the press when Keiko played with pods but did not connect with them, "Right now he's just hanging around—like taking you to Japan and saying, 'O.K., man, make friends and feast out.'" The fact remains that Keiko enjoyed the freedom from which he would otherwise have been deprived, especially if Wometco Enterprises had had their way.

While Luna and Lolita waited for agencies and activists to work together so that both members of L pod could be returned to their natal waters, on December 17, 2003, U.S. District Judge Robert Lasnik ordered NMFS to reconsider listing the Southern Resident population as endangered, giving the organization twelve months in which to do so. Lasnik criticized the agency for failing to rely on the most up-to-date scientific information available, saying, "To deny listing of a species simply because one scientific field has not caught up with the knowledge in other fields does not give the benefit of the doubt to the species and fails to meet the best available science requirement." Lasnik ruled that there was no support for fisheries' scientists' conclusions that the potential extinction of the Southern Resident population would not create a significant gap in the overall species, which they had hypothesized would be repopulated by offshore and transient orcas. According to the classification system known as taxonomy, established by Carl Linnaeus in 1758, there is only one species of orca in the world. More than two centuries later, biologists have recognized there are three separate populations in the eastern North Pacific Ocean—resident, transient and offshore—each exhibiting different genetic and behavioral characteristics.[41] While the federal review was underway, on April 3, 2004, Washington State Department of Fish and Wildlife listed all Salish Sea orcas as "Endangered."

A year after it was instructed to reconsider the decision, NMFS announced that the Southern Residents *would* receive protection under the ESA. The agency proposed to list them as "Threatened" while a public comment period was underway, and the agency worked toward putting final protections in place.

One facet of nature the free-ranging Southern Residents were unlikely to need protection from was the threat of hurricanes. This was not the case for Lolita, who has endured the onslaught of nature's wrath for many years with little or no protection. The danger of hurricanes poses a perpetually serious threat to the Florida coast, and the potentially lethal effects on the Seaquarium and its occupants cannot be underestimated.

While 2004 was one of the costliest Atlantic hurricane seasons on record, with the Seaquarium suffering wind damage to signs and roofing, sea wall erosion and sediment-filled pools, 2005 was set to create even more havoc with the arrival of Hurricane Katrina in late August. Four days before Katrina hit the Gulf Coast, the hurricane struck south Florida as a Category 1 storm.

Described as "the deadliest hurricane to strike the U.S. since the Palm Beach-Lake Okeechobee hurricane of September 1928,"[42] the eye of the storm passed directly over the Seaquarium between Key Biscayne and the mainland, sinking boats, damaging buildings and blowing down trees and power lines east and west of the park. Three days later, 27 percent of Miami-Dade County was still without electricity.

The Seaquarium, which was closed for three days, remained tight-lipped about any damage. No news reports surfaced to document the effects of the storm on the marine mammals and other animals at the park. The rim of the tank holding Lolita is about fifteen feet above sea level, well under the twenty-to-thirty-foot storm surge that Katrina pushed ashore along the Gulf.

The Marine Life Oceanarium in Gulfport, Mississippi, an infamous dolphin sales and rental agency, was demolished by Katrina. Some captive dolphins survived the onslaught of the hurricane, only to be swept out to sea when the storm surge overwhelmed their tank. Naomi Rose, speaking for HSUS, warned that this could happen again if the aquarium was rebuilt in the same place. It never was, and now only the ruins remain.

With the tail-end of Katrina's power and force still fresh in everyone's minds, two months later, on October 24, further devastation followed in Katrina's wake when Hurricane Wilma swept through Florida, leaving yet another trail of destruction with winds clocked at 116 miles per hour on Key Biscayne. The force severed power to 98 percent of Miami-Dade County and Broward County. Trees were downed, and parts of the Seaquarium were flooded in addition to damage inflicted on the sea wall. Although none of the park's marine mammals was injured, fifteen sharks and one thousand fish were killed, necessitating the park's closure.[43] In the absence of any direct reports regarding Lolita's welfare, it was assumed that she had, once again, miraculously survived nature's fierce onslaught.

While the park remained closed for essential repairs and little knowledge of Lolita's status was known, following many years of advocacy, Lolita's family was at long last granted the protection to which it was entitled. On November 18, 2005, with the newly recognized knowledge that orcas live in culturally distinct communities, NOAA Fisheries listed the Southern Resident orcas as endangered. But there was a sting in the tail. Included in the final rule was this paragraph:[44]

Captured orca in Penn Cove, 1970. *Terrell C. Newby, PhD.*

The Southern Resident killer whale DPS does not include killer whales from J, K or L pod placed in captivity prior to listing, nor does it include their captive-born progeny.

It was a cruel and crushing blow for Lolita. Not only had she been denied her freedom, but the powers that be also decreed that she was to be denied the protection afforded to the rest of the Southern Resident population. Her exclusion from the listing effectively closed the door on any potential lawsuits that could be brought on her behalf under the ESA.

Following a sixteen-week closure, the Seaquarium reopened on February 11, 2006. The additional havoc created by the hurricane could not have come at a worse time. Attendance had still not recovered from the post-9/11 economic downturn. "You don't see the South Americans coming and staying for months at a time as you did before," said Hertz. The park had fallen almost $2 million behind in rent payments on its county-owned site while funding a costly three-year renovation effort mandated by the county in 2003. Hertz claimed the storm cost the Seaquarium $2.5 million in damage plus over $4 million in lost revenue. The overall costs, according to Hertz, totaled approximately $8.5 million.[45]

The park's refurbishment included a new dolphin program called Dolphin Harbor, home to ten Atlantic bottlenose dolphins, featuring a 12,000-square-foot, 700,000-gallon dolphin pool surrounded by an 8,000-square-foot amenity, including a reception area, education seminar room, changing facilities and rest rooms. The Seaquarium stated that the new attraction was part of a long-term plan to shift its focus away from the animal shows and allow a more interactive experience for visitors. Dolphin Odyssey, in which participants can swim with dolphins and allow themselves to be towed along holding on to the dolphin's dorsal fin, and Dolphin Encounters, whereby people can shake hands or share a friendly kiss with dolphins with no swimming involved, are offered. For $495, it's possible to be a trainer for a day.

While Lolita returned to her usual routine of performing twice daily, another member of her pod met his fate. Fears for Luna's safety were realized on March 10, 2006, when he was killed by a 104-foot-long tugboat that had taken shelter in Nootka Sound. Although Luna frequently approached the wash of props, the tugboat was larger than those to which he was accustomed. As the boat idled with Luna lagging in its wake in his constant quest for companionship, the capricious juvenile fell victim to the rotating blades. The death of a young, healthy male was yet another devastating blow to the Southern Resident community. Two years later, both his mother and the sister he never knew disappeared within a few weeks of each another.

THE CURSE OF CAPTIVITY

Over the years, celebrities offering to support the Lolita campaign have come and gone. In November 2007, Garrett received a surprise call from a person claiming to be Mexican actor/philanthropist Raul Julia-Levy, son of Puerto Rican actor Raul Julia (Raúl Rafael Juliá y Arcelay, 1940–1994). His widow denied Julia-Levy's paternity claim, saying that he was an impostor.

"Lolita's already made her captors millions of dollars. How much is enough? Greediness has its limits and it is time Lolita goes back to her family. We need to make Lolita's voice heard." Julia-Levy's rousing words boosted Garrett's hopes, injecting the Lolita campaign with fresh energy. The actor promised to contact Hollywood's rich and famous and put Garrett on the phone with actor/screenwriter Jean-Claude Van Damme. Within days, Julia-Levy had drawn up an impressive list of stars, including actors Johnny Depp, Hayden Panettiere, Harrison Ford and game show host Bob Barker. Although the effort generated a lot of publicity for about a year, Garrett had no contact with any of the celebrities. Gradually, like others before them who had vowed support for Lolita, the big names faded from the scene, and Garrett distanced himself from Julia-Levy.

From the beginning, the Free Lolita campaign had been one of hope and expectation marred by disappointments and setbacks. Undeterred, Garrett and Berta, who were now married, continued to pursue the campaign in Washington State while a well-informed and dedicated environmental science psychology major, Shelby Proie, took up the cause in Miami. Proie organized regular protests and demonstrations outside the Seaquarium, and in October 2008 was interviewed for a four-minute segment about Lolita that was shown on CNN every hour throughout the day. Another short documentary titled *Saving Lolita*, produced by Jenny Cunningham of PBS's KCTS 9 TV for KCTS Connects, aired the same month.

With no shortage of media wanting to tell Lolita's story, in March 2009, a short 3-D animated film titled *Perchance to Dream*, produced by student Lauren Kimball (Solace Skies Productions), was released. Kimball's inspiration for the film came while researching how to improve her ability to animate animal movements. She had been taken to see Lolita when she was a child, an experience that troubled her. She relays Lolita's story in scenes from Lolita's world, her memories of home and dreams of rejoining her family versus the reality of life in a cramped tank performing circus acts. Kimball plays to the audience's imagination by asking what happens in Lolita's mind when the lights go off and the tourists depart. The film received critical acclaim, and Kimball received the Golden Flamingo Award under the Viewers' Choice category at the 2009 South Beach International Animation Film Festival, Miami. It was accepted into the Blue Ocean Film Festival in Georgia and shown at the short film corner of the world-famous Cannes Film Festival in France. Kimball also designed the logo for an international day of protest held around the world on May 15, 2010, for Lolita's retirement.

Another documentary titled *The Cove* made headline news that summer. Directed by former *National Geographic* photographer Louis Psihoyos, the film reveals the shocking truth about the Japanese town of Taiji. Using covert filming methods, Psihoyos and crew, including O'Barry, exposed the barbaric slaughter that takes place from September to March, when hundreds of dolphins are driven into a picturesque cove. The water runs red with blood as innocent victims are rounded up and slaughtered for meat, while the most attractive ones are destined to a lifetime in captivity. *The Cove* premiered at the 2009 Sundance Film Festival in Utah and was later nominated for an Oscar for Best Documentary Feature by the Academy of Motion Picture Arts and Sciences. That summer, O'Barry joined the Penn Cove commemoration protest outside the Seaquarium, as he had done many times before after renouncing all affiliation with captivity.

That subject was now well and truly at the fore. It would make Christmas 2009 a particularly painful one for the family and friends of twenty-nine-year-old killer whale trainer Alexis Martinez, who was employed at Loro Parque theme park/zoo in Tenerife, Spain. On Christmas Eve, a day spent by many preparing for one of the most important dates on the ecclesiastical

"Captivity kills." Ric O'Barry protests at Miami Seaquarium. *Orca Network.*

calendar, Martinez was violently killed by Keto (b. 1995), a 6,600-pound orca on breeding loan from SeaWorld, Orlando. Martinez's body was recovered from the bottom of the pool by SeaWorld trainer and supervisor Brian Rokeach. Rokeach himself had been subjected to the unwelcome attentions of Orkid, another of SeaWorld's orcas, when the whale grabbed him by the leg and held him underwater for almost half a minute.

Martinez's death, which took place during a Christmas show rehearsal, barely made the press until two months later. On February 24, 2010, one of the most shocking events in marine park history took place when experienced trainer Dawn Brancheau was killed and mutilated at SeaWorld, Orlando, by Tilikum, who had killed twice before. The industry rocked as the news broke and rippled across continents.

Profoundly affected by the shock of Brancheau's horrific death and angered by the spin SeaWorld put on the story (which initially claimed that Tilikum grabbed Brancheau by the ponytail, thus placing the onus for safety on the trainer), within days, a number of former SeaWorld trainers, including Jeffrey Ventre, John Jett, Carol Ray and Samantha Berg, spoke out. As Balcomb commented in relation to another orca incident at Seaworld,

San Diego, when Kasatka attacked trainer Kenneth Peters, "In captivity they're dangerous because they're big and sometimes they're not happy with their situation. In the wild they're not dangerous to humans and there are no incidences of them attacking humans unprovoked."

The controversy surrounding Brancheau's death led to an investigation by OSHA that resulted in a $75,000 citation against SeaWorld for three safety violations, one of which was classed as willful, a violation committed with plain indifference or intentional disregard for employee safety health for "exposing its employees to hazards when interacting with killer whales." A second citation, classified as "serious," was levied for failing to install a stairway railing system on one side of a stadium stage; a third citation involved a failure to put weatherproof enclosures over outdoor electrical receptacles.[46] The company contested the fine, which was later reduced to $38,500.

But despite attempts to minimize the bad publicity emanating from Brancheau's death, SeaWorld could not stem the tide of suspicion arising from the tragedy. Two investigative journalists, Tim Zimmerman (*Outside Magazine*) and David Kirby (*Death at SeaWorld*), began their own probes into the deadly attack. In the summer of 2010, together with Ventre, Jett, Ray and Berg, they met with marine mammal researchers and others, including Garrett and Balcomb, in a private house on San Juan Island. Suzanne Chisholm and Mike Parfitt, producers of *Saving Luna* (later remade under the title *The Whale*), were present, along with film producers Gabriella Cowperthwaite and Manny Oteyza, who had just started work on a low-budget documentary titled *Blackfish*. The documentary, which premiered at the 2013 Sundance Film Festival in Park City, Utah, on January 19, 2013, drew international acclaim, pulling back the curtains hiding the dark secrets of captivity to reveal the sordid, ugly truth. It would have an unparalleled effect on the public's perception of orca captivity and seriously jeopardize SeaWorld's reputation and business. The low-key meeting of the minds on San Juan that summer was the first gathering of "Superpod," an event that has become widely known and is now attended by scientists, filmmakers, naturalists and activists from around the world who support cetacean freedom.

While the investigation into Brancheau's death was in progress, Lolita was again in potential danger. The Gulf Coast Deepwater Horizon BP explosion on April 20, 2010, started in the Gulf of Mexico from a drilling platform and continued for eighty-seven days. It remains one of the worst environmental disasters the world has ever seen, with 210 million gallons

Superpod attendees watch whales from Center for Whale Research. *Richard Snowberger.*

of oil affecting five Gulf Coast states, including Florida. Three months later, on July 15, National Public Radio (NPR) reported that, although the threat of the oil spill carried on the Gulf's loop into the Atlantic Ocean had diminished, a change in currents, wind patterns or, at worst, a hurricane, could bring disaster to the occupants of the Seaquarium. With a daily intake of 10,000 gallons of water from Biscayne Bay, the park's management team was looking at options, including wells, to augment the water supply. Although Florida Keys, Miami-Dade and Broward beaches are more at risk from big spills than anywhere in the state outside the Panhandle, South Florida escaped the spill.[47]

Having survived the threat of another potential disaster as the oil slick made its way down the coast, Lolita's plight was again brought to the public's attention with the second annual Walk for Lolita taking place in numerous venues, including Miami and Seattle.

Lolita would also gain extra publicity when television commercial director Daniel Azarian produced *Save Lolita*, a ninety-second public service announcement. The PSA uses the same kind of emotional technique and tone, visually and musically, that effectively promotes human causes like Save the Children. "I wanted to appeal to people who might not understand how unethical Lolita's situation is by presenting her predicament through human eyes," Azarian explained. Azarian, who graduated with honors from New York University's Tisch School of the Arts, pursued his career at Warner Bros. marketing home video releases. His filmmaking abilities won him three 2008 Telly Awards, including Telly's highest honor, the Silver Award, for his futuristic-themed cosmetic spot, "Bulletproof," for Facez Cosmetics. He directed and produced national spots for 3M's Scotch-Brite brand and Horizon Organic; blue-chip telecommunications firms and entertainment networks have licensed Azarian's commercial spots for their U.S. and international mobile networks. *Save Lolita* won the director two 2011 Telly Awards and was selected for the opening night at the Hamptons Conservation Wildlife Film Festival and the New York Wildlife Conservation Film Festival. Azarian also was a finalist in the 2012 Blue Ocean Film Festival. The PSA helped raise publicity for Lolita's cause on

Friendly gray whale Baja. *Richard Snowberger.*

Miami's NASCAR Championship racetrack Jumbotron, where it played once every hour for each of the twelve hours on each of the three days of the races—a total of thirty-six times.

Time off is a rarity for Lolita. She is by far the biggest draw at the Seaquarium (surveys have shown that two out of three ticket-buyers come to see her); days off from performing cost the park money. But early in March 2011, Lolita had an unexpected break from her monotonous routine.

Just before Garrett was scheduled to join Orca Network's annual gray whale trip to Baja, Mexico, the Whale Bowl unexpectedly closed for a week. Rumors circulated that the tank was under repair and that Lolita had a toothache. With so much uncertainty surrounding Lolita's health and the possibility of a media storm, Garrett canceled his upcoming trip to wait for news. No further details emerged from the park except that Lolita was on antibiotics, until Garrett received a firsthand report that Lolita had performed in a scheduled show with trainers riding on her back. Following the recent OSHA citation against SeaWorld regarding safety issues, the ruling should have sounded a warning bell to the Seaquarium. Although Lolita had never seriously injured a trainer, there was always the possibility that the frustrations created by her isolation in the cramped tank, her loneliness and boredom could suddenly trip a switch with potentially devastating results.

10

TRIALS AND TRIBULATIONS

With the tide of public opinion turning and the reputation of a large corporation tarnished, on October 26, 2011, the first of a series of lawsuits advocating for the rights of captive cetaceans was brought on behalf of five SeaWorld orcas—Tilikum, Katina, Corky, Kasatka and Ulises—when the largest animal rights organization in the world, People for the Ethical Treatment of Animals (PETA) Inc. joined O'Barry, Visser, Garrett, Berg and Ray against SeaWorld Parks & Entertainment Inc. and SeaWorld LLC. The suit was based on the Thirteenth Amendment to the Constitution of the United States, which prohibits slavery and involuntary servitude.[48]

It was a valiant effort to apply an integral part of the U.S. democracy to non-human entities, even though U.S. District Judge Jeffrey Miller dismissed the case on February 8, 2012, saying, "The only reasonable interpretation of the Thirteenth Amendment's plain language is that it applies to persons, and not to non-persons such as orcas."

Although the suit failed, both sides voiced one shared observation, namely the remarkable nature of the animals. Judge Miller praised PETA attorneys for striving to protect orcas, but still found that the Thirteenth Amendment "affords no relief." Despite the case's dismissal, it succeeded in drawing attention to how orcas, like humans, suffer from confinement and domination.

As Garrett has expressed many times, dolphins of all species (the orca is the largest member of the dolphin family) exhibit a truly wide array of

Statue of Liberty, New York Harbor, New York City. *Wikipedia.*

behaviors, but in nature, they do not for a minute exhibit the sedentary life of a captive orca or dolphin. In natural conditions, they travel, forage, play, socialize, spy-hop, breach, lob-tail and engage in hundreds of uncategorized activities that never cease. They don't sleep as we know sleep. They need to stay awake to actively control the timing of each explosive breath or drown. There is no provision in the highly evolved dolphin behavioral repertoire for staying still. It's entirely unnatural and leads to weakened metabolisms and compromised immune systems, often leading to opportunistic infections and death.

Former dolphin trainer Laura Singer had expressed a wish back in 1999 for an attorney to take on Lolita's case. Now, many years later, her wish was about to become true.

NMFS SUED FOR VIOLATION OF ADMINISTRATIVE PROCEDURE ACT

On October 27, 2011, a day after the case against SeaWorld was filed, PETA, ALDF and three other plaintiffs (Shelby Proie, Karen Munro and Patricia Sykes) served notice of intent to sue NMFS, alleging that the agency had violated Section 4 of the ESA when it excluded Lolita from the listing of the Southern Residents in November 2005. In a recovery plan dated January 17, 2008, NOAA stated:

> *One Southern Resident whale...known as Lolita...remains alive in captivity at the Miami Seaquarium. Efforts have been made to raise support to relocate this whale to the wild and reunite her with the Southern Residents, although captive release efforts involving one killer whale...and other delphinids have been largely unsuccessful.*

The agency added that, as Lolita was captured in 1970, before the introduction of the MMPA in 1972, "She does not fall under the jurisdiction of NMFS."[49]

Following the ruling, on November 17, 2011, ALDF, PETA and the individual plaintiffs filed a further lawsuit against NMFS for violation of the Administrative Procedure Act (APA) of 1946, arguing that regulatory exclusion from the ESA listing of captive Southern Resident orcas was illegal.[50] "Lolita was torn from her family...exploited for every dollar the Seaquarium can squeeze out of her and finally betrayed by the government agency charged with protecting her. This regulatory 'gift' to an industry notorious for making orcas' lives miserable is not only incredibly cruel but blatantly illegal," were the words of Jeffrey S. Kerr, general counsel for PETA.[51]

The judge dismissed the case on procedural grounds on May 1, 2012, ruling that the plaintiffs had not complied with the ESA's requirement that citizens must provide the government with sixty days' notice before filing suit. The plaintiffs appealed, contending that the government had received the required notice of intent to sue and the case was, therefore, wrongly dismissed.

USDA Sued for Renewing the Seaquarium's License

Year in, year out, the USDA has without fail renewed the Seaquarium's exhibitor license for Lolita. Two months prior to its expiration in April, ALDF wrote to the USDA alleging that Lolita's living conditions were inhumane and that renewal of the license would be unlawful. Elizabeth Goldentyre, eastern regional director of APHIS, replied that the USDA would renew the license, as the Seaquarium was in "compliance with the regulations and standards."

PETA, ALDF, Orca Network and private citizens disagreed with Goldentyre's opinion. On August 22, 2012, they filed a complaint against the USDA for declaratory and injunctive relief in the U.S. District Court for the Northern District of California for routinely renewing the Seaquarium's license.[52] "It shouldn't take a lawsuit to force the USDA to stop handing out permits to the smallest orca tank on the continent," said PETA Foundation director of captive animal law enforcement Delcianna Winders. "PETA and ALDF are calling on the government to give Lolita her long-overdue freedom from misery, isolation, and exploitation."[53] The Northern District of California granted the Seaquarium's motion to intervene and the USDA's motion to transfer the case to the Southern District of Florida.

Petition to NMFS to Delist the Southern Resident Orcas

Human nature being what it is, there will always be those driven by their own personal and business interests who endeavor to change the status quo for their own ends. Almost seven years after the Southern Residents were listed as endangered, NMFS received a petition dated August 1, 2012, submitted by the Pacific Legal Foundation seeking to delist the endangered Southern Resident killer whale DPS. The petitioners claimed that the killer whale DPS did not constitute a listable unit under the ESA, as NMFS is without authority to list a DPS of a subspecies, and that there was no scientific basis for the designation of the unnamed North Pacific Resident subspecies of which the Southern Resident killer whales were purportedly a DPS. The petition also presented new information regarding genetic samples and data analysis pertinent to the question of discreteness and the DPS determination. Three months later, on November 27, NMFS made a ninety-day finding accepting the petition, based on the additional genetic samples and publication of new peer-reviewed scientific journal articles regarding the taxonomy of killer whales, and requested information to initiate a status review.[54]

The timing of the petition to delist the Southern Residents was particularly odious in light of the pending appeal against NMFS for failing to include Lolita under the ESA. If protection were to be removed from the Pacific Northwest orcas, there would no longer be a case for Lolita to be protected as a member of the group.

In an effort to settle the case, on October 14, 2012, PETA and ALDF agreed to hold the appeal against NMFS in abeyance. In exchange, NMFS would consider a new petition to extend the protection granted in 2005 to cover members of the Southern Residents and their offspring in captivity at the time the protection was granted. NMFS was required to decide, within ninety days of the petition being filed, if it presented substantial commercial or scientific information indicating that the petitioned action was warranted. If so, a full review would begin.

If the agency made a final decision within twelve months of the filing, the parties would move for voluntary dismissal of the action. The plaintiffs requested that, regardless of the outcome, NMFS go on record with a final decision, and a rationale for same, within the specified time period. "This important step means that NMFS must hold to the legally required time frames that the agency often ignores and cannot let ALDF's and PETA's petition to secure Lolita the protection to which she is entitled languish indefinitely," said Carter Dillard, ALDF's director of litigation.

PETITION TO NMFS TO INCLUDE LOLITA IN ESA LISTING

Following the settlement, on January 23, 2013, PETA, ALDF, Orca Network, Howard Garrett, Shelby Proie, Karen Munro and Patricia Sykes petitioned NMFS to revise the endangered species listing of Southern Resident killer whales by removing the exclusion of captive whales from the description. The agency was required to make its initial finding "to the maximum extent practicable, within ninety days after receiving the petition."

Three months later, on April 29, NMFS published this statement in the *Federal Register*: "We find that the petition, viewed in the context of information readily available in our files, presents substantial information indicating the petitioned action may be warranted." The agency would now have nine months in which to reach a decision, including a ninety-day comment period.[55]

Following the comment period, NMFS dismissed the petition brought by the Pacific Legal Foundation to delist the Southern Resident population, determining that "the Southern Resident population is discrete and significant with respect to the North Pacific Resident subspecies and therefore constitutes a valid DPS....We conclude that the original data for classification were not in error and delisting is not warranted." The insidious attempt to remove the Southern Residents from their protected status had created an anxious twelve months for orca advocates, and the agency's decision was welcomed with considerable relief. It also gave rise to fresh hope for Lolita's future inclusion under the ESA.

In response to the petition submitted by PETA and others to include Lolita as a member of the endangered Southern Resident killer whale DPS, after completing a status review, NMFS proposed to amend the regulatory language of the ESA listing of the DPS by removing the exclusion for captive members of the population, pending a two-month comment period commencing January 27, 2014, although it would still take up to a year before any rule was made final. Over nineteen thousand comments were filed, most of them favoring Lolita's inclusion under the ESA. Many of the comments urged that Lolita be returned to the Pacific Northwest and eventually released back to the wild.

Lolita's life story has always been one of trials (now in the most literal sense) and tribulations. Whether by sheer coincidence or otherwise, that same day, Wometco Enterprises chose to announce the sale of the Miami Seaquarium to California-based Palace Entertainment, which is owned by Spanish-based Parques Reunidos. According to its website, the conglomerate operates more than sixty different assets, including theme parks, zoos, marine and water parks and other entertainment centers around the world, mostly in Europe and the United States. Despite Hertz's declaration that there would be no change in Lolita's status, it was impossible not to wonder how she might be affected by the transition.

CASE AGAINST USDA DISMISSED AND APPEALED

While progress had been made in one direction, stalemate was reached in another when, on March 18, 2015, a Florida federal judge dismissed ALDF's case against the USDA challenging the legality of renewing the Seaquarium's license to display Lolita. The case was dismissed on the grounds that the inspectors have the discretion to ignore the regulations written by Congress, in essence, the USDA can renew licenses even if the conditions violate the AWA.

While lawyers and advocates teamed up to weigh the scales of justice in Lolita's favor, a permanent reminder of her history, and that of her family, was literally launched in her home waters. Popular with commuters and visitors alike, the Mukilteo/Clinton ferry, which runs between the mainland and Whidbey Island, is the shortest of the Washington State Ferry routes, with a crossing time of approximately twenty minutes. With a ferry based at each dock, the two pass each other mid-channel several times daily. If orcas are in the vicinity of the ferry lanes, the boats must stop and wait for them to go by. Many a passenger has been thrilled to hear the captain announce that whales are on the port or starboard side.

There could not be a more fitting tribute to Lolita than naming a new vessel after her and, on June 8, the official unveiling of the *Tokitae* took place. The name was originally proposed by Whidbey Island children's author Deb Lund in 2010; her father-in-law, Vern Olsen, remembers only too well the 1970 Penn Cove capture and hearing the whales' piercing cries. Although not chosen then, the name ranked in the top five submitted. Now proposed again by Orca Network, the name came in as the number one choice. Support came from people in forty-four states and thirty-three countries, including trainers who knew Lolita/Tokitae and had worked with her. The name was in keeping with the tradition of giving ferries tribal names and would honor Tokitae and the many other orcas that suffered and died as a result of the capture era.

Washington State ferry *Tokitae. Author collection.*

Tokitae nameplate. *Author collection.*

Tokitae ferry bell. *Author collection.*

OSHA CITES MIAMI SEAQUARIUM

Meanwhile, a time bomb was ticking away in Miami. Despite the recent OSHA ruling against SeaWorld, trainers continued to do water work with Lolita. Stephen Wells, the executive director of ALDF, filmed the late afternoon show in May and submitted the video to OSHA. ALDF had previously sent a formal letter to OSHA in November 2013 seeking enforcement of standards to protect workers from captive orcas at the Seaquarium. Although no action was taken then, following an inspection on July 10, 2014, the agency issued a citation and notification of penalty (OSHA complaint No. 867630) that same day. OSHA stated in its letter to Wells that, during the inspection, a number of trainers were observed interacting with Lolita in manners that "were found to present a struck-by and/or drowning hazard for the animal trainers." A penalty of $7,000 was proposed, the violation to be abated by August 26, 2014.[56]

"We celebrate OSHA's swift enforcement against this dangerous facility," Wells responded when hearing the news. "The Miami Seaquarium is risking trainers' lives to exploit Lolita, a wild-captured orca, for huge revenue. The corporation continues to disregard worker safety and animal welfare laws as long as it brings in big profits." Despite initially saying that it would appeal the fine, the Seaquarium settled and agreed to keep trainers out of the water. Lolita would no longer be ridden like a surfboard.

The Seaquarium suffered further bad publicity after former law enforcement officer Steven Bagenski and two other activists filed suit through the American Civil Liberties Union (ACLU) of Florida for violation of First Amendment rights following Bagenski's arrest in August 2014, when he was held by Miami-Dade Police Department for displaying a "Free Lolita" sign while standing on a public sidewalk.[57] The regular protests outside the Seaquarium had become tenser following the police department limiting demonstrators' access to over forty feet of the public sidewalk, referred to as the "red zone." This meant that demonstrators had to stand back from the entrance and exit on an area designated the "green zone," reducing their ability to distribute leaflets or talk to visitors entering the Seaquarium, resulting in some ugly confrontations taking place between police and protestors. In addition to getting rid of the red zone policy, the county paid Bagenski $1,330 to settle the case.[58]

While lawsuits stacked up in the courts, there was no let-up in public and media pressure on the Seaquarium. On January 17, 2015, the biggest demonstration to date took place with the Miracle March for Lolita when around 1,500 people from across the world converged on Miami, congregating near the Seaquarium. Garrett traveled from Whidbey Island to speak at the event, hoping to see Lolita and check on her welfare. It had been many years since he had last seen the whale whose freedom he had championed for so long. But it was not to be—his hopes of seeing Lolita were dashed when he was stopped by officials in the Seaquarium parking lot and denied entry.

Following an agonizingly long wait, two years after the submission of PETA's petition to NMFS to include Lolita under the ESA, NMFS determined that "captive members of the Southern Resident killer whale population should be included in the listed Southern Resident killer whale DPS." Finally, on May 11, Lolita was officially designated as endangered along with the rest of her family and afforded the protection that had so wrongfully been denied her.[59]

PETA and Others Versus Seaquarium for ESA Violations

PETA seized the moment, giving the Seaquarium sixty-day notice of intent to sue under the ESA. Lolita's enhanced status would in some ways act as a double-edged sword—while offering her much-needed protection, it would also be used as a propaganda tool by her masters for protecting the species and keeping her a prisoner.

USDA Appeal Denied

While PETA prepared its case, on June 17 the appeal brought on July 1, 2014, against the USDA for issuing a license to the Seaquarium was denied. An even more explicit statement was delivered by the Eleventh Circuit Court of Appeal in Atlanta that the Seaquarium need not be in compliance with the AWA to continue being licensed. Judge Susan Black ruled, "Congress has not directly spoken to whether the USDA can renew a license despite knowing that an exhibitor is non-compliant with animal welfare standards." Once again, Lolita fell victim to the machinations of the law and agency interpretation.

Soon after the ruling, with the expiration of the sixty-day notice of intent to sue the Seaquarium under the ESA, on July 20, PETA, ALDF, Howard Garrett and Orca Network filed suit against the Miami Seaquarium and Festival Fun Parks LLC, D/B/A Palace Entertainment, for violating the ESA.[60] The case, brought to the U.S. District Court, Southern District of Florida, alleged that Lolita was being harmed and harassed in violation of the "take" prohibition of the ESA, in essence, the Seaquarium "confines Lolita—a highly intelligent, social and complex individual—to a small, shallow and barren concrete tank, without adequate protection from the sun, and without a single orca companion." Among other pleadings, the plaintiffs claimed relief for 1) unlawful take of a Southern Resident killer whale and 2) unlawful possession of a taken Southern Resident killer whale. They requested that the Seaquarium forfeit possession of Lolita and transfer her to a sea-pen in accordance with an established rehabilitation and retirement plan. Now that Lolita enjoyed the federal protection that had eluded her for so long, surely this was a case that could not possibly fail?

11

DARKNESS FALLS

Undeterred by the failure of the lawsuit and appeal against the USDA for renewing the Seaquarium's license, in May 2016, PETA, ALDF, the Orca Network and Garrett filed a fresh suit against the USDA in U.S. District Court, Eastern District of North Carolina (where the headquarters of the Animal Welfare Operations for the eastern region of the USDA and APHIS is based) for violating the AWA by granting a license to the Seaquarium's new parent company, Palace Entertainment.[61] The plaintiffs claimed that, under the act, licenses are not transferable after there has been a change in ownership and that licenses can only be granted to facilities in compliance with the USDA regulations. Jared Goodman, PETA Foundation director of animal law, stated that "Miami Seaquarium's new owner simply does not qualify for a permit for this facility, when the orca confined there is suffering in an illegally small concrete pit." It was another shot across the bows of the agency that had persistently failed to interpret the regulations in a way which would help Lolita and improve her dire situation.[62]

After almost a year of depositions, exchange of documents, attempted mediation and an inspection of the proposed sea-pen site on Orcas Island, on June 1, 2016, U.S. District Judge Ursula Ungaro dismissed the case brought against the Seaquarium for violations of the ESA. Ungaro ruled that the conditions in which Lolita is kept, and the injuries the plaintiffs presented to the court, were largely addressed under the AWA and not under the ESA. According to the ruling, until Lolita's captivity can be shown to *gravely threaten* her survival, the ESA had not been violated.

"We were definitely surprised by this decision, based on an incredibly narrow and, we believe, flawed interpretation of the ESA," Goodman stated. He added that Ungaro had interpreted the act to not protect captive endangered animals from anything but imminent death, for which there is no basis in the law.

It would not be the first time Ungaro had courted controversy within the legal system. Born in 1951, she graduated from the University of Miami in 1973 with a bachelor of arts degree and from the University of Florida College of Law with a juris doctor in 1975. Appointed as Ursula Ungaro-Benages, she was involved in a scandal in 2003 when allegations of a sexual affair between herself and a key witness, former Royal Canadian Mounted Police investigator William Majcher, were made while Ungaro was ruling in the case of Vancouver lawyer Martin Chambers, who was sentenced to fifteen years in prison for money laundering for a Colombian drug cartel.[63]

Although Ungaro noted in her summary judgment that the plaintiffs' expert witness opinions about Lolita's medical conditions had a "speculative and unreliable quality," she ordered certain documents to be unsealed, including the depositions of the plaintiffs' four expert witnesses: veterinarian Dr. Pedro Javier Gallego Reyes, based in Luxembourg; former senior SeaWorld trainer and author of *Beneath the Surface*, John Hargrove; Dr. Ingrid Natasha Visser, Orca Research Trust, New Zealand; and Dr. Maddalena Bearzi, president of Ocean Conservation Society, based in California. The statements make disturbing reading.

Reyes, Hargrove and Bearzi carried out an on-site inspection of the Seaquarium and Lolita's conditions on January 20, 2016, for approximately nine hours, between 4:20 a.m. and 1:12 p.m. (Bearzi conducted her inspection between 7.00 a.m. and 1:10 p.m.) Visser attended the Seaquarium in 2013 and 2015 to monitor Lolita's conditions.

Reyes, Hargrove, Bearzi and Visser had access to the Seaquarium's animal behavior records from 2001 to 2015. The records give details of interactions between Lolita and the trainers, including relationships, husbandry, shows, play, training sessions, food, behavioral ratings for each session and medications. Records for the years 2005, 2007 and 2008 were missing. It was Hargrove's understanding that the Seaquarium had either destroyed or misplaced those records. Visser noted missing animal behavior records for the week June 22 to 28, 2015, and all of the behavioral records for December 2015.

Despite his years of working in the captivity industry, on entering the stadium Hargrove expressed shock at the size and shallow depth of Lolita's tank. Visser had reacted similarly in 2013 with the words, "I knew this was small, but this small? When you actually see it you realize how tragically small that tank is," when she visited the Seaquarium for the first time with Daniel Azarian to make the documentary *A Day in the Life of Lolita, the Performing Orca*. Hargrove stated, "Lolita's tank at Miami Seaquarium is without question the smallest and most barren I have ever seen an orca forced to live in." Although the tank holds 580,496 gallons of water, according to the Seaquarium, records indicated that the water level was often dropped.

Hargrove noted that, during the time he was at the stadium, the only form of enrichment Lolita had, and showed any interest in, was sitting at what appeared to be the inflow valve (which was most likely introducing concentrations of highly chlorinated water) where she floated motionless at, or just under, the surface. The only times she left the spot during the inspection period was when trainers and employees entered the stadium prior to the park opening, when interacting with trainers and when chasing took place between herself and the Pacific white-sided dolphins. When preparations for the show were underway, she continued to float motionless at the inflow valve. Hargrove stated that such abnormal repetitive behavior was indicative of intense boredom and lack of enrichment.

Lolita's only other forms of enrichment are, as previously mentioned, a wetsuit, some floats and a dribble of water from a hose. In addition to the danger of the wetsuit being an ingestion hazard, which could cause Lolita's death, Hargrove witnessed trainers using the garment to play tug-of-war with her. According to the Seaquarium's records, on occasions Lolita had failed to give the wetsuit back to her trainer.

Lolita is on a cocktail of drugs. She is often heavily medicated with antibiotics (Baytril, clavamox, amoxicillin and cephalexin) to prevent, or treat, infection from raking by the Pacific white-sided dolphins. The records supplied showed that Lolita had been raked more than three hundred times by her companions. Bearing in mind that records for more than three years were "missing," how many more times has she been raked?

Tramadol, a painkiller, is also administered. Although she is post-reproductive, records show that Lolita is given Regu-Mate, a form of birth control. This drug was used for a trial period at SeaWorld but stopped due to dangerous side effects. According to Hargrove, it was handled by a male trainer wearing latex gloves, as it can cause infertility in female trainers. In postmenopausal whales, the drug is used as medication to treat ovarian cysts, endometriosis, cancer, endometrial polyps and polycystic ovarian syndrome.

Lolita's "toy" wetsuit. *Ingrid N. Visser, Orca Research Trust.*

In addition, ranitidine, a drug used to treat ulcers caused by stress, fluconazole to treat fungal infections and Simplicef to treat skin infections are given.

Eye drops, including prednisone, are regularly put in both eyes, which are documented as "cloudy." Her right eye has a pterygium, also known as "surfer's eye," a syndrome caused by dust, low humidity and excessive exposure to UV radiation. Symptoms of pterygiums include tearing, dry and itchy eyes, foreign body sensation and inflammation; they can also cause considerable alteration in visual function.

Records show that Lolita often keeps one or both eyes closed during shows. In 2015, she was given eye drops every single day, and on every day except four in 2014 (often twice). Hertz disregarded the installation of shade for Lolita on the grounds that APHIS had advised that too much shade can lead to pathogen build up, costly structural alterations might be necessary and "shade may necessitate fundamental changes in how Lolita (Tokitae) is exhibited and allowed to interact with her professional trainers and the public."

During her inspection, Bearzi noted that blisters, wrinkles and sunburns on Lolita's skin were recorded in the animal behavior records. She also monitored the various sources of noise to which Lolita is exposed, which, during her inspection, included "persistent and loud anthropogenic noise caused by construction, pumps, airplanes, people passing by, audience and music, trucks and cars."

Chasing by the Pacific white-sided dolphins was documented more than 150 times. Lolita's behavior was described as "anxious or agitated" more than 50 times.

Over 250 occasions of head-bobbing were recorded. Hargrove qualified the context of this behavior in his report: "She had a high number of head bobs when she would fail on a behavior during the delivery of a Least Reinforcing Scenario (LRS)....If the animal remains calm for this pause… sometimes, but not always, there is an opportunity for reinforcement." Hargrove noted that Lolita often demonstrated frustration at failing and "exhibited the aggressive precursor of head-bobbing," including, as he witnessed, head-bobbing when the veterinarian swabbed her teeth on the day of the inspection. Trainers documented more than 300 times when Lolita was "tense" and "extremely tense" on numerous occasions.

Jaw-popping is another stress indicator and a precursor to aggression. This behavior was documented eight times in the records. Lolita has also pushed a trainer into the pool, attempted to bite a trainer's leg and lunged toward a visitor with her mouth open.

Drilling (a procedure known as pulpotomy) of one or more of Lolita's teeth (the records did not specify which tooth or how many) was carried out for five days in April and a further three and five days in May 2011. There was no respite for her from the show following the pulpotomy procedure—still medicated and with her tooth, or teeth, actively bleeding, she was expected to perform. The show went on after her teeth were drilled on May 21 and stomach and blood samples were taken, although not without some sign of protest from Lolita when she head-bobbed a trainer. She was also forced to perform while medicated for a dental abscess in February 2009 that caused bruising and swelling to her lower jaw viz: "2-27-2009—abscess in right side of mouth; two shows and full sessions carried out with trainer in water; also some evident precursors of aggression (tense)."

She is not pulled out of shows when dolphins have raked her so that she has time to heal. In 2015 alone (minus five weeks of missing records), at least thirty-four entries were recorded in twenty-one separate weeks referring to "rakes," for example, on August 10, 2015: "Three new rake marks on chest and belly, rub above L pec." On 109 days in 2004 rakes (up to two feet long), bites and other lesions were found.

Rubs, sores and abrasions were frequently observed. Because of the severe space restrictions, Lolita's flukes drag along the bottom of the tank, and her rostrum and pectoral fins are continuously in contact with concrete surfaces. The animal behavior records showed that she had rubbed various parts of her body more than 350 times. Trainers had recorded "rubs all over body" no fewer than 5 times.

Records showed that gating was often used to separate Lolita and the dolphins, usually in the main part of the tank (A) but sometimes in the back (B). On at least two occasions in 2002, the water level dropped seven and nine feet. In 2015, Lolita was gated overnight for almost a month in total for different reasons. Here are a few examples:

> 1) *5-11-2015 MSQ3706: large scrape observed on Lolita's pectoral fin; she displays pattern swimming throughout the day; she is given tramadol medication. Lolita gated overnight in A.*
> 2) *1-7-2015 MSQ3742: new rakes by lags on her ventral side and dorsal fin. Lolita gated overnight in A.*
> 3) *10-31-2003 MSQ9223: water dropped three feet; Lolita and Pacific white-sided dolphins gated in A for two and a half days.*

As stated by Reyes, every animal display facility has a commitment to three basic principles: education, conservation and research. In his opinion, the Miami Seaquarium's program contained misinformation and, as far as he was aware, had neither contributed to the conservation of wild orcas nor produced any significant research in relation to killer whales. From his observations, he concluded there was clear evidence that the management and training personnel lacked specific orca husbandry skills.

In his summing up, Reyes stated, "We are potentially dealing with a patient with a chronic pulmonary disease, decreased kidney function, possible stomach ulcer(s) and recurring dehydration. This does not represent an animal which should be performing every day in repeated shows."

In her summary conclusion, Visser stated, "It is clear that Tokitae is generally lethargic, that she consistently exhibits an apathetic behavioral state in which her stupor is displayed to the point of her being basically catatonic for much of the time."

In the face of such damning evidence, it is difficult to comprehend how any judge could dismiss the case on the grounds given.

When considering Lolita's suitability for release, it is important to remember that these ailments are created by unnatural confinement in a cramped space for so long and the perpetual harassment from the Pacific white-sided dolphins.

Following the hearing, PETA and co-plaintiffs asked the Eleventh Circuit to reverse Ungaro's ruling, arguing that the lower court used the wrong standard to determine that Lolita's conditions were not considered a "take" under the ESA. They asserted that Ungaro erred in her judgment when ruling that a captive animal is not "taken" unless the animal is subjected to conditions that gravely threaten its life. The proper standard, they claimed, was that Lolita was subject to both "harm" and "harassment" by being confined in an undersized tank without adequate protection from the sun or compatible companionship.[64]

The appeal was supported by the HSUS. The society said that rather than decide that the AWA was the controlling statute, Ungaro should have used the AWA as a baseline standard of welfare for animals in captivity in addition to the extra protections provided for ESA-listed species.

PETA also argued that summary judgment was inappropriate because issues of fact remain as to Lolita's alleged injuries and her living conditions. Although the evidence provided to support claims of Lolita's injuries was redacted from the brief, the information regarding her health was produced pursuant to a protective order but not made public.

While the arguments continued to rage, following years of constant denial by the USDA/APHIS that Lolita's tank was illegal, the Marine Mammal Commission (MMC) announced in August 2016 that the tank *was* substandard.

Following APHIS's February 2016 notice (81 Fed. Reg. 5629) proposing to amend its regulations by implementing the AWA as those regulations pertained to marine mammals, the MMC took APHIS to task, citing a similar discussion paper in 1991. "It is particularly disappointing that now, twenty-five years later, APHIS has done nothing to follow through on this recommendation and has opted not to address the minimum space requirements under S. 3.104," said Rebecca J. Lent, executive director.

Earlier, *Miami New Times* reported that a statement issued by APHIS confirmed that the measurements for the required minimum space for marine mammals are taken without obstructions. Lyndsay Cole, assistant director of legislative and public affairs for APHIS, stated, "The minimum horizontal dimension (MHD) is calculated for only those areas of the pool that are unobstructed and meet the depth requirements." Obstructions such as the concrete island in Lolita's tank (it is not a floating platform) mean that she cannot "posture" herself naturally. The tank does not, therefore, satisfy the four factors (depth, volume, surface area, MHD of forty-eight feet) to comply with the law.

Not long after Cole made her statement, APHIS representative Tanya Espinosa, a public affairs specialist, told *Miami New Times* that obstructions such as the concrete work island *were* allowed, providing they were not detrimental. She did not say who decides when an obstruction is "detrimental," nor did she qualify any specific regulations allowing such obstructions.

The MMC cited Section 3.104(a) of the space regulations, concluding that "the Commission does not believe that APHIS has met those requirements with either the current or proposed regulations. All minimum space requirements should be met in an unobstructed manner, otherwise the definition of 'minimum' would be rendered meaningless." The commission recommended that APHIS clarify that all minimum space requirements for all species/groups under Section 3.104 be calculated and based "on unobstructed horizontal distances and depths" in its final rule.[65]

Espinosa named Dr. Elizabeth Goldentyre, the director of the agency's eastern region, as the person who oversees the compliance of Lolita's tank. According to Espinosa, it is Goldentyre's opinion that the AWA allows for obstruction.

In response to a letter written by Sacramento-based Wendy Cooke in June 2011 complaining about the size of Lolita's tank, Goldentyre replied that "shade and protection from weather is provided by the stadium seating around Lolita's pool" despite aerial photographs showing the entire tank exposed to direct sunlight.[66]

Despite Cooke and others pursuing the matter with the USDA's Office of Inspector General (OIG), the stalemate continued.

Now, faced with censure by the MMC, Espinosa conceded that Goldentyre, along with other APHIS officials, *might* change her opinion on whether the concrete wall in Lolita's tank was "detrimental" to the orca's well-being and whether it violated all of the space requirements. "The proposed rule explicitly did not include changes to the space requirements or the way they are calculated," said Espinosa. "APHIS will continue to review the issue of space requirements for further action.… We will then consider our next steps."

Rector was stunned that APHIS officials might change their minds, especially since he has been urging them to do so for years with little success. He credited Lent, the director of the MMC, as being the motivation for Goldentyre's apparent mulling over whether Lolita's tank was compliant with the spirit of the law. He expressed concern, however, that Goldentyre might ponder the issue indefinitely and make no decision or take any action.

When asked why space requirements were not brought up in the proposed rule, Espinosa replied, "APHIS does not have sufficient scientific or other supporting data to support increased space requirements at the time; however, we will consider any new data provided on this issue during the comment period or later."

But in June 2017, a report released by the USDA Office of the Inspector General found that the Whale Bowl may not be in compliance with the AWA after all.[67] The audit revealed that "the design of the enclosure may deny the resident orca sufficient space for adequate freedom of movement." Although the Seaquarium was not directly named in the report, both the photos of the enclosure and its dimensions correlate with those of the Whale Bowl. The report specifically cited a tank with only one orca—Lolita is the only solitary captive orca in the United States. The USDA's representative had visited the facility between October 2015 and August 2016, and the audit had focused on seven parks, four of them based in Florida.

Despite this damning evidence of noncompliance, quoting from the USDA's letter to the Seaquarium in 1999, Andrew Hertz maintained that the Whale Bowl "meets the intent and the letter of the law with regard to space requirements for orcas."

Sometimes, while the wheels of justice turn with slow and painful precision, an unforeseen natural disaster can change the course of events. If Ungaro's ruling that Lolita's life had to be *gravely threatened* before her case could be considered under the ESA, then such a possibility became a real threat with the savage onslaught of Hurricane Irma in September 2017.

The phenomenon of Irma began on August 30, 2017, near the Cape Verde Islands off the west coast of Africa, rapidly intensifying to a Category 3 hurricane. On September 4, Irma became a Category 5, with winds reaching 185 miles per hour on September 6. Although the storm abated for a while, it reached Category 5 status yet again before making landfall in Cuba. After once again dropping to Category 3, the storm gathered strength once more to a Category 4 hurricane as it hurtled relentlessly toward Florida. Rick Scott, the governor of Florida, declared a state of emergency and gave the order on Friday, September 8, to close all colleges and public schools statewide that day and the following Monday. By the evening, hundreds of thousands of residents had evacuated their homes. Miami International Airport, among others, ceased operating by late Saturday.

Now, instead of hearing the scream of jets overhead, Lolita would be subjected to the howl and roar of the wind and the bang and clatter of flying, scattering objects. With a predicted storm surge of ten to fifteen feet at Florida's southern tip and above nine feet along the west coast, she would await her fate as, along with Walt Disney World Resort, Universal Orlando Resort and SeaWorld Orlando, the Seaquarium closed its doors. While dolphins in Cuba were airlifted to safety by helicopter before Irma made landfall and zoos and other marine parks in Florida moved their animals to provide some degree of protection, no such provision was made for Lolita and the other marine mammals. When asked why it had not taken its animals to safety, the Seaquarium stated,

> *Miami Seaquarium has been at its present location since 1955 and it has withstood its fair share of storms. The park has an experienced and dedicated team working diligently to ensure our animals are safe. In preparation for the possible effects of Hurricane Irma, Miami Seaquarium has implemented its hurricane preparation procedures....You can monitor our social channels for all updates regarding the park.*

However, no updates were available on social media channels either before closing the park or during the storm, nor was there any explanation as to the precise nature of the procedures the leadership claimed to be putting in place for their animals during hurricanes. Equally important, there was no clarification as to whether staff were to remain on-site as Irma hurtled toward Florida. Lolita and her companions had no choice but to face the fury of the fast-approaching monster. If it stayed on its present path, the storm would pass right over the Seaquarium.[68]

Although Lolita, as an endangered orca, is entitled to the protection of NMFS and APHIS is required to have an emergency contingency plan, the latter has made no attempt to enforce the AWA emergency contingency plan requirements in the past.

The biggest concerns surrounding Lolita's survival centered on flying debris from the park. The stadium roof, which had the potential to twist in the wind and blow into the tank, was especially high-risk. The velocity of the storm was more than likely to take out the power operating the filtration and refrigeration systems keeping the water in her tank cool, to say nothing of the potential storm surge that could compromise the dozens of construction jacks placed every few feet under the tank to support it. In that eventuality, the tank could split or tip. If the rumors were true that two personnel planned to stay at the park as the storm ran its course, dealing with any such devastating damage was clearly beyond their capability.

Not only was the Seaquarium itself under threat, but when interviewed, the mayor of Key Biscayne expressed his concerns about the structural integrity of the Rickenbacker Causeway Bridge providing road access to the Seaquarium. In the event that the bridge sustained substantial damage or was demolished, access to the Seaquarium and subsequent repairs would be delayed.

As the eye of the storm moved toward the coast, Miami braced itself for the full impact of nature's wrath. With the Rickenbacker Causeway closed and the Seaquarium isolated, Lolita and her companions would have to weather the storm as best they could.

No one knows what Lolita endured as the full force of the hurricane struck. For many hours, she was subjected to life-threatening destruction all around her. In Garrett's words, "Now we wait for news about Lolita like thousands of family members in a hospital waiting room, fearful but hopeful." While the storm churned and raged, the world watched, waited and wondered.

Against all the odds, Lolita survived, although had the storm not changed course and veered about ninety miles to the west of Miami, she might not have done so. As had been its modus operandi in the past, the Seaquarium remained silent regarding the welfare of the animals in its care. It was not until Lincoln O'Barry, Dolphin Project, flew a drone over the Whale Bowl on September 11 that confirmation of Lolita's status was obtained. She appeared to be alive, a pitiful sight lying in murky water, seemingly alone in the empty stadium still standing in the flooded theme park. As O'Barry said, "It looks like she's swimming in a cesspool." Just what did it take to qualify the court ruling that, until Lolita's captivity can be shown to *gravely threaten* her survival, the ESA has not been violated?

According to Ceta-Base, an organization that records the acquisition and deaths of marine mammals in captivity, seven of the Seaquarium's Nile crocodiles (one of nature's toughest species) were killed and two bottlenose dolphins died in the aftermath of the hurricane. In the wild, dolphins have been known to swim to deeper waters ahead of storms, an option not possible for those in captivity.[69]

The Seaquarium remained closed for a month after the passage of Irma, reopening on October 13 with the offer of huge discounts. While the Flipper Stadium and Discovery Bay were still closed for repairs, it was back to work for Lolita.

The second appeal following the dismissal of the lawsuit for violation of the ESA by keeping Lolita, a member of an endangered species, in "abusive conditions" was heard on December 4, 2017. PETA attorney

Delcianna Winders took up Lolita's case before Eleventh Circuit Judges Susan Black, Frank Hull and visiting U.S. Court of International Trade Judge Jane Restani. The judges were asked to decide whether Lolita was being harmed or harassed by looking at three factors: AWA compliance, whether the animal husbandry practices are generally accepted and the likely risk of injury. Winders argued that the Seaquarium's compliance was disputed, while the Seaquarium argued the *gravely threatened* standard had been correctly applied.[70]

Appeal of ESA Case Dismissal Dismissed

But on January 12, 2018, the Eleventh Circuit Court of Appeals in Miami did not find in Lolita's favor. Despite claiming that Lolita's enforced confinement at the Seaquarium constituted "harm" and "harassment" under the definition of "take," which is illegal under the ESA, and citing thirteen separate injuries to Lolita as per the veterinary and expert witness inspections, the judges upheld the lower court ruling that, by keeping Lolita in captivity, the Seaquarium was not in violation of the ESA. After seeking to define the terms *harm* and *harassment* under the ESA and interpreted in accordance with *Webster's Third New International Dictionary 1034 (1986)*, the court concluded that "the evidence, construed in the light most favorable to PETA, does not support the conclusion that the conditions of her captivity pose a threat of serious harm to Lolita."

In response to the judges reasoning that "accounting only for the dictionary definitions of 'harm' and 'harass' would bring (minor) annoyances to endangered animals that bear no reasonable relationship to extinction within the ESA's coverage—a result inconsistent with its purpose," Garrett commented, "The appellate court has determined that kidnapping and forcing Tokitae into involuntary servitude, in essence, slavery, is only a minor annoyance that doesn't even amount to harm or harassment under the ESA." Goodman, PETA's director of animal law, told the press, "This ruling sentences this highly intelligent, deeply lonely and distressed orca to a lifetime of physical and psychological harm, confined to a tiny concrete cell without family, friends or freedom."

PETA FILES PETITION FOR PANEL REHEARING AND FOR REHEARING EN BANC

Although it seemed that further recourse through the courts was exhausted, a relatively unknown avenue remained open. On February 2, 2018, PETA, ALDF, Howard Garrett and Orca Network filed a further petition against the Miami Seaquarium and Festival Fun Parks LLC d/b/a Palace Entertainment for rehearing en banc (an appellate court may grant a rehearing *en banc*—a French term meaning "on the bench," where judges usually sit while hearing cases—to reconsider a decision of a panel or court, generally consisting of only three judges when a case concerns a matter of exceptional public importance or the panel's decision appears to conflict with a prior court decision).[71] PETA urged that the court should not be concerned with aggressively interpreting the ESA "because Congress intended the ESA to provide protections for endangered animals." Lolita's future was once more in the hands of the judicial system and how the powers that be chose to interpret the law. But on October 9, 2018, the federal appeals court rejected the petition to reopen the lawsuit on the grounds that there was no threat of serious harm that could trigger a federal animal welfare law violation. The court also stated that it could not identify a "realistic means" of returning Lolita to the wild without her being harmed. Yet again, despite the protection afforded under the ESA, the law courts had failed her.

HOPE FOR THE FUTURE

Legal battles are not the only battles being fought on Lolita's behalf. Her cause has now been taken up by one of the biggest and strongest federally recognized ocean-based Coast Salish tribes, the Lummi Nation (Lhaq'temish—the People of the Sea), whose hereditary chief and chief of council is Bill "Tsilixw" James. Original inhabitants of Washington's northernmost coast and southern British Columbia, traditionally, Lummi settled and occupied sites in the San Juan Islands and now live to the west of Bellingham, south of the Canadian border. As hunters and fishers since time immemorial, their culture and survival depend on salmon.

The Lummi people first heard about Lolita's story after a young woman from upstate New York contacted them. She kept dreaming that Tokitae was trying to communicate and heard her calling, "Can anybody hear me, can anybody help me go home?" The dreams were so vivid that she contacted Douglas James, an elder of the Lummi Nation. He took her claims seriously and talked to others on the tribal council, who undertook their own research. After members of the tribal council completed their study and a group of transient orcas swam past his grandmother's house in Bellingham Bay, council member Nickolaus Dee Lewis contacted Garrett and asked, "How can we help?"

On August 1, 2017, the Lummi Nation passed a motion supporting the campaign to bring Lolita home. In a letter addressed to Garrett dated August 7, the Lummi Indian Business Council announced,

S/V *Cutty Sark* and *Suva*, Penn Cove commemoration, 2017. *Author collection.*

S/V *Cutty Sark* at Penn Cove capture site. *Author collection.*

Left: Susan Berta plays the Native American flute in memory of the whales. Penn Cove 2017. *Author collection.*

Below: Members of the Lummi Nation embrace the dark memories of Penn Cove. *Author collection.*

Howard Garrett recalls the captures on S/V *Cutty Sark*. *Author collection.*

The Lummi Nation honors our connection to the Killer Whale (qw'e lh ' ol mé chen) as a culturally significant species and supports the work of the Lummi Nation's Sovereignty and Treaty Protection Office in its efforts to bring the Killer Whale Tokitae home to her family as soon as possible.

In Native American society killer whales are spiritual beings and an intransigent part of their culture. In the same way as the Mowachaht Nation revered Luna as the reincarnation of their chief, Tokitae is the Lummi Nation's ancestral sister and daughter. Like Tokitae, many of their children were kidnapped and forced to abandon their culture. To the Lummi Nation, freeing Lolita from the Miami Seaquarium is a "sacred obligation" in accordance with their 1855 treaty rights under the U.S. Constitution, which gives them the legal right to fish in usual custom areas and protect fish and coastal lands.

One of the ways in which the Lummi Nation has expressed its influence and shown support for environmental issues has been by the ancient art of totem pole carving. Master Carver Jewell "Praying Wolf" James of the Lummi Nation's House of Tears Carvers learned traditional carving from his family as a child. Among many other creations, James has carved

Lummi Island and Mount Baker, Washington State. *Richard Snowberger.*

traditional healing poles, including one for the families and friends of victims of the September 11, 2001 attack on the Twin Towers in New York City. He exhibits his respect for the ancient western red cedar trees by blessing them in a prayer ceremony. A single totem pole can take up to one thousand hours for the master carver and his team to complete. James announced early in 2018 that his next carving project would be a totem pole in honor of Tokitae, to represent the trauma she has endured and the resilience she has shown in surviving. When completed, the Tokitae totem pole would be transported across the country to Miami, accompanied by the powerful trailer to a future documentary produced by Geoff Schaaf and Dennie Gordon.

Gordon, a successful director in great demand who graduated from Yale School of Drama, New Haven, Connecticut, initially gained recognition in 1994 for her script *A Hard Rain*, which was chosen by Showtime's Discovery Program. The film went on to win awards at the British Short Film Festival and the Hamptons International Film Festival.

After completing his MA at California State University, Schaaf exercised his talents making documentaries around the world, receiving a total of four Emmy awards and thirteen Emmy nominations.

Tokitae Totem Pole with Master Carver Jewell James. *Nickolaus Dee Lewis.*

The nine-minute, high-impact trailer, which includes scenes of Lolita's proposed sea-pen at Glenwood Springs Salmon Hatchery on Orcas Island, was shown at a press conference hosted by Philip Levine, former mayor of Miami Beach (who was running for governor of Florida, a bid that failed), at Levine campaign headquarters in Miami on March 12. Just before he resigned to begin his campaign, and in the aftermath of Hurricane Irma, Levine and his city commission issued a resolution urging the owners of the Seaquarium to retire her. He also wrote to Fernando Eiroa, president and CEO of Parques Reunidos, urging him to move Lolita.

Opening the press conference, Levine quoted Mahatma Gandhi: "The greatness of a nation and its moral progress can be judged by the way its animals are treated," while Lummi Council chairman Jeremiah "Jay" Julius reiterated the tribe's mission to bring Lolita home.

Garrett was also present at the press conference and referred to the transport and retirement plan for Lolita's return, based on Balcomb's original plan introduced in 1995:

1. *Professional staff will train and prepare Lolita to position herself in a sling.*
2. *She will be examined by a team of veterinarians for overall health and any communicable pathogens. Appropriate permit applications will be submitted.*
3. *Lolita will be led by her current caretakers into the stretcher and lifted by crane into a water cradle on a truck trailer.*
4. *The truck will carry Lolita in her water cradle to Miami-Dade International Airport, and load her into a cargo aircraft to Bellingham International Airport, Washington State. She will be accompanied by her trusted caretakers at all times.*
5. *Upon arrival by truck to Bellingham harbor, the truck will be driven onto a barge and towed to her sea-pen in Eastsound, Orcas Island.*
6. *A crane on the barge will lift Lolita in her sling and lower her gently into the seawater in her sea-pen. At this point, she will once again swim in her natal waters and will be known again as Tokitae.*
7. *Tokitae will be cared for in her sea-pen until she consistently demonstrates good health records for a period acceptable to her consulting veterinarian.*
8. *With the consent of veterinary and scientific staff, Tokitae will begin boat-recall training (in the same way as Keiko) to respond to an acoustic signal within the sea-pen. During this time, she should demonstrate the ability to forage effectively on live fish while fresh and dead fish remain available.*
9. *Boat-recall training will take place outside her sea-pen in a larger, temporary pen.*
10. *After Tokitae has regained her metabolic strength and stamina and continues to demonstrate her competence to forage, she will be allowed free range of the Salish Sea.*
11. *A permanent care, companionship and provisioning station will be staffed and maintained at a location familiar to her, available at any time she chooses.*

Despite assurances that, like Keiko, Lolita would be free of pathogens before any transfer to Puget Sound, questions regarding Lolita's survival still arose. Garrett accepted that these were of legitimate concern. As he has explained many times before, it may be hard to accept that Lolita likely has a vivid memory of her home waters and family life unless it is understood that orcas are highly advanced in cognitive and associational abilities, which also means immense memory retention, probably beyond normal human capacities. While in the womb, orcas can hear their family and are well developed when born. They know how to swim at birth and are using their calls in a couple of months. Lolita learned her pod's calls way before her first birthday as well as how to catch fish. She traveled with her family for at least three to five years, by which time she had learned her family's language and traditions and the skills needed to survive. She knew who she was. Neuroscientist Dr. Lori Marino provides the brain science to back that up. "The adult brain is the most convoluted brain on earth, and the orca forebrain comprises a greater proportion of the total brain volume than does the human forebrain. The neocortex is greatly expended, particularly in areas of 'integrative' higher-order processing of emotions and social cognition."[72]

Garrett summarized, "I think that's all firmly retained in her memory. But the most important aspects of their lives are their family, their clan. They learn what and what not to eat, learn the rules. I really believe that she will remember them. Lolita has the ability to catch fish."

Despite requests by the tribal council to arrange a meeting, the Miami Seaquarium wrote on March 6 that "Lolita will continue to be an ambassador for her species from her home at Miami Seaquarium, educating park guests on the plight of the endangered Southern Resident Killer Whales of the Pacific Northwest."

This is not the view of the Lummi Nation, who consider Lolita an ambassador for the Salish Sea. During a three-part series filmed by news anchor Louis Aguirre for Miami's Local 10 ABC News, Aguirre took his crew to Orcas Island to talk to both Balcomb and Jim Youngren, owner of the Chinook salmon hatchery at the site of the proposed sea-pen that would provide Lolita with her daily food ration. Youngren started Glenwood Springs Salmon Hatchery in 1978; the hatchery produces thousands of salmon and releases 750,000 salmon a year back into the Salish Sea.

Balcomb explained that the sea-pen location for Lolita's retirement is ideal for many reasons. The water is deep, and there is an embayment that can be penned off. Initially, she would be contained in a small pen that can be opened up to a larger one after she has had time to acclimate to her new surroundings. She would once again feel the sway of the currents and explore the kelp beds that orcas find so intriguing. A small island acts as a natural barrier to protect the site, which is on land that used to be an ancient Lummi village. Now the Lummi have entered into a Memorandum of Understanding with Youngren to buy the 160 acres surrounding the cove, regardless of whether Lolita is moved there or not.

A bald eagle watches over the Salish Sea. *Author collection.*

Orca with salmon in the Salish Sea. *Center for Whale Research.*

Like the Lummi Nation, Balcomb considers Lolita to be an ambassador for the Salish Sea. Global warming, disappearing salmon, pollution and shipping congestion have all wreaked havoc on the delicate ecosystem. Lolita's return is part of the plan to draw attention to the repair of that ecosystem before it is too late.

While concerted efforts to persuade the Seaquarium to release Lolita continued, the subject of the Southern Residents was high on the agenda in Seattle at the Daybreak Star Cultural Center. On March 14, 2018, Governor Jay Inslee signed Executive Order 18-02 to implement immediate actions to benefit the Southern Residents. The immediate actions, some of which were to be effective by the end of April, include enforcement of vessel and fishing regulations in orca areas, oil spill training for whale watch boats and adjustment of commercial and recreational fishing regulations. It was proposed that measures for quieting ferries in areas frequented by the Southern Residents be developed by May 31. By July 1, existing outreach resources should be prioritized, and by July 31 watersheds and marine areas, which would enable action to be taken to help get more prey for the whales, must be identified. By December 15, Chinook salmon recovery projects should be assessed. A demanding, but essential schedule.

The order included assembling a Southern Resident killer whale task force to formulate a longer-term action plan addressing the major threats to the whales. Working with its neighbors in Canada, the group would report to the governor by November 1, 2018. Ironically, it was at this same venue that Balcomb made a speech in March 1995 announcing the launch of the Lolita Project to clean up and maintain the marine waters of Puget Sound as a healthy and productive environment for humans and whales.

As the executive order was rolled out to provide much-needed relief for her family, Lolita performed one of her two shows of the day before a spectator who had championed her cause for over twenty years. Garrett, wearing a wide-brimmed hat and sunglasses, managed to gain entry to the Seaquarium. He admits to feeling nervous that he would be stopped in the parking lot as he was during the 2015 Miracle March for Lolita. No doubt he was observed by Seaquarium staff, but with such intense media scrutiny focused on Lolita, perhaps they decided it was better not to risk attracting further adverse publicity. Garrett was heartened, in as much as he could be, to see that Lolita's energy was high as she swam around the tank, breaching four times, and that she appeared to have a good relationship with one of the trainers in particular.

After the show, Dr. Kurt Russo, the Lummi Indian Business Council's political strategist, had the following conversation with Robert Rose when he asked if he could speak to Lolita:

> *Russo: "Can I say hello to her?"*
> *Rose: "No."*
> *Russo: "I can't say hello to her?"*
> *Rose: "No. But you can say hello to me."*
> *Pause…*
> *Russo: "So where's she from?"*
> *Rose: "You know* exactly *where she's from."*

Following a blessing ceremony in Bellingham on May 9 heralding the start of the Tokitae Totem Pole journey to Miami, many people along the route also learned exactly where Lolita was from. The 197-year-old cedar redwood, carved into a sixteen-foot totem pole in the likeness of an orca with two eight-foot seal poles at the base, underwent further blessing ceremonies in Washington State before stopping in Oregon, California and Texas, arriving in Florida on May 21. Each event hosted local tribal entities, accompanied by singing, dancing and words of wisdom from individual

Lolita waits for food. *Howard Garrett.*

Kurt Russo, Lummi Nation chief strategist, asks to speak to Lolita. *Howard Garrett.*

speakers. Attendees were invited to lay their hands on the totem pole and impart their spiritual strength and prayers for Lolita as the totem pole journeyed across the country.

The vibrantly colored totem pole is a work of art. Two salmon are carved on each side of the whale, representing the Southern and Northern Resident orca population's principal diet; on either side of the whale are two human figures, one looking up, the other looking down. Two raven heads, another important part of Native American mythology, are depicted on the tail end. Two seals at the base of the totem pole represent the staple diet of the transient orca population. The Whale Rider sits resplendent behind the whale's dorsal fin. Mythologically, he or she is taken below the water to join his/her ancestors.

With a forecast of torrential rain and thunderstorms, the team braced itself for a wet and windswept weekend. Florida had already had more than the usual rainfall for May with heavy downpours and surface flooding. Weather stations were monitoring the threat of a potential tropical storm heading toward Miami.

Garrett and Berta arrived in Miami on May 24. While the couple were traveling, the trailer carrying the totem pole parked strategically in front of the Miami Seaquarium. There could be no ignoring the powerful message, while inside the park a multimillion-dollar renovation was underway with a new retro-modern entrance that includes a gift shop, an interactive touch pool and a new flamingo exhibit. But there is still no sign of a new tank for Lolita. The only change there is a new Jumbotron.

In June 2003, a Miami-Dade legislative entry mentioned $5 million in lease payments from the Miami Seaquarium and stated that "the Corporation has finished the design and plans for a new Marine Mammal Habitat (the "Project") that will cost approximately $20 million."[73] When asked 1) whether or not the plans were submitted to the planning department and, if so, when? and 2) if they were submitted were they approved and, if so, what was the date of that approval, the reply by the chief of the Regulatory and Economic Resources Zoning and Public Works Plan Review Division read, "I have not seen a permit application for a marine mammal habitat. A permit application was submitted for improvements to the ticket office."[74] Just as Dr. John Hall forecast in the 1998 documentary *Lolita: Spirit in the Water*, in twenty years' time, there would still be no new tank.

Garrett and Berta both visited Lolita during their time in Miami. Berta describes the experience as bittersweet. After the show, as he stood at the end of the perimeter fence surrounding the tank, Garrett pulled up the hood of his rainproof jacket to reveal the bold slogan "Bring Lolita Home." By then, it was too late to eject him from the stadium.

As torrential rain fell over much of Florida and impending tropical storm Alberto drew closer, the governor of Florida announced a state of emergency. It did not deter those who had traveled to Miami from congregating at the Miami Circle in downtown Miami. The archaeological site, discovered in 1998, measures thirty-eight feet in diameter and has twenty-four basins ranging from one to three feet cut into the limestone bedrock, located close to the water's edge. The basins are believed by some experts to depict the images of manatees, dolphins, sea turtles and other marine species, and to have been built by the Tequesta Indians. The Circle's historical connection to the indigenous people was, therefore, of particular significance as an appropriate venue for the final part of the totem pole journey. As the clouds burst and the moist, warm wind rose and rushed through the tree tops, taking out the live stream and microphones recording the event, Berta exclaimed, "The sky is crying."

Later in the day, during an address at Florida International University hosted by Canadian actor Adam Beach, a member of the Saulteaux First

Nations best known for his role as Victor in *Smoke Signals* and with many other credits to his name, Freddie Xwenang Lane of the Lummi Tribal Council sent a warning message to Rose in response to his recent claim during a news interview that the Lummi do not care whether Lolita lives or dies.

> *I say to you Mr. Rose, because I know you have your people watching at the Seaquarium. You don't know Lummi people. You should understand that we have powerful allies. In just this past week Northwest Indians passed a resolution of more than fifty Native American tribes signing on to bring Lolita home…we will be back.*

The morning of the rally on May 27 dawned wet and forbidding. Miami was under a tornado alert with a warning to seek shelter. Those who had undertaken this special journey gathered in a marquee near the Seaquarium. As Lane addressed the crowd, the wind tore at the canvas while curtains of rain swept by, swamping the sodden ground. Despite the raging elements, there was no doubting the resolution, determination and energy as, led by the Blackhawk singers chanting ancestral songs, the procession set off in the howling wind toward the marine park. Aguirre and his camera crew covered the story while Schaaf continued filming. As the group lined up on the sidewalk, the wind abated and a ray of sunshine broke through the clouds. Looking up at the sky, Lane thanked the Creator and handed Lolita's future over to him. Miami-based Carib Indian Tribal Queen Catherine Hummingbird Ramirez, who regularly performs Native American ceremonies for Tequesta Indians at the Miami Circle, had her own words for Lolita as she offered a prayer: "It's Tokitae, not Lolita. We are crying here right now for Tokitae." For the Seaquarium, she had other words: "We will call up the Great Spirit as we stand here grieving to send Lolita back home. You stole her from her family, from our family, we want her back now."

Garrett enjoyed a special moment in time as he looked across the street to where Lolita waits for her freedom. Placing a recording device up to the megaphone, he played Lolita's family calls. At exactly the same time, people in Washington State following the live stream were interrupted by a different call. Alisa Lemire-Brooks, Orca Network's sightings coordinator, notified orca watchers that a pod of transient orcas was again in Puget Sound. The pod had been reported the previous day near Whidbey Island when the event at Florida International University was underway. For two days running, while the intensely emotional scenes played out in Miami, orcas were in the vicinity of Lolita's capture location.

As the calls faded, Lane addressed the fortress housing Lolita. "Is there anyone from the Seaquarium here today? We're here to tell you we love Lolita. We have our elders right here. We're asking you to come talk with us."

For a few seconds, it seemed as if time stood still. The silence was rudely broken by a cacophony of loud music emanating from the marine park, ending as abruptly as it began when news crews panned in on the scene. Grim-faced, the deputation to bring Lolita home played her family calls once more before turning to leave. The attempt to discuss Lolita's future with the Seaquarium had failed; as Jewell James summed up during a recent interview, "We can do this the easy way or the hard way." The Seaquarium, it seems, had made a choice.

EPILOGUE

Donald Goldsberry, the man who captured Lolita, died in 2014. He was never to redeem himself by carrying out the undertaking he signed on May 28, 1996, in which he stated that, having consulted with Balcomb regarding the safe transport of Lolita from Miami to the Pacific Northwest, should an agreement be reached to retire or return her to her native waters, he would provide the expertise and assist with the arrangements to move her in return for no payment except his meals, accommodations and transportation. Included in the undertaking was this sentence: "I originally caught Lolita in Penn Cove in August 1970 and sold her to the Miami Seaquarium." His partner, Edward "Ted" Griffin, a man without remorse, is still alive and living in eastern Washington.

Former dolphin trainer turned activist Russ Rector died in his sleep at the age of sixty-nine on January 7, 2018.

Palace Entertainment named Eric Eimstad as general manager of the Seaquarium in February 2018, replacing Andrew Hertz.

Fernando Eiroa, CEO of Parques Reunidos, resigned in October 2018.

Tilikum, snatched from his family as a calf in 1983, died at the age of thirty-five on January 6, 2017, at SeaWorld, Orlando. What would his legacy be? A "killer whale" who took the lives of three humans or a tortured soul driven to psychotic behavior by an existence confined to a concrete tank from which there was no escape?

In 2006, NOAA fisheries announced a research project to recover the skeletal remains of the young orcas killed during the 1970 Penn Cove capture in hopes of finding, through DNA testing, some answers to the decline of the Southern Residents. More than ten years later, the skull of an orca calf is one of the exhibits at Orca Network's Langley Whale Center on Whidbey Island, serving as a permanent reminder of a tragedy still remembered by many. The tiny skull was discovered and cared for by a Coupeville resident who witnessed the horror of the captures. Orca Network board member Sandy Dubpernell arranged for it to be reconstructed as completely as possible by the Burke Museum. A couple of bony fragments were sent to a laboratory that can isolate DNA, and the remaining pieces have been archived. The DNA material was sent to Kim Parsons at NOAA for further analysis in the hope that she can determine gender and to which pod the calf belonged. It may take some time for the results of the testing to be released, as Parsons has to wait until she has enough samples to make the test feasible financially and time-wise. The spirit of the orca calf was blessed by Samish Nation tribal elders Rosie Cayou and Bill Bailey in a moving ceremony at the 2016 Penn Cove commemoration.

The "Blackfish effect," as it has become known, has been largely attributed to the decline in attendance at SeaWorld parks and the rapid fall in the company's stocks. It created such a backlash of negative public opinion against SeaWorld that, with profits continuing to plummet, SeaWorld made an unexpected and surprising announcement in November 2015 that it would be changing its business model. After fifty years of displaying orcas, the corporation stated its intention to end orca entertainment shows (replacing them with "educational" shows) in San Diego, California, at the end of 2016. Other shows at Orlando, Florida, and San Antonio, Texas, will be phased out by 2019. It would make no difference to the lives of the orcas already in captivity at SeaWorld, as many of them have worn-down teeth from chewing on the sides of the tank and could not survive in the wild. The only alternative for those whales is transfer to a sea-pen or sanctuary—similar to the proposal for Lolita. The Whale Sanctuary Project, which was initiated at a meeting in Vancouver, British Columbia, in 2015, aims in brief to develop seaside sanctuaries to rehabilitate whales and dolphins so that they might live out the rest of their days in an environment as close to their habitat as possible.

Legislation to ban orca captivity and breeding in the United States was initiated on March 16, 2017, with the introduction of Federal Bill H.R.1584. The Orca Responsibility and Care Advancement Act of 2017 was sponsored by Adam Schiff (D), representative for California's Twenty-Eighth Congressional District. The bill aims to amend the MMPA to

Blessing of orca spirit by Samish elder Bill Bailey. *Sandy Dubpernell.*

prohibit taking, importing or exporting orcas and orca products for public display and for other purposes but permits exportation of a killer whale to a marine mammal sanctuary. It also proposes to amend the AWA to prohibit any person from artificially inseminating or breeding killer whales with the intention of using their progeny for public display purposes and is in the first stage of the legislative process.

In Florida, the Orca Protection Act HB 1305 was introduced in the Florida House of Representatives by Representative Jared Moskowitz (D) on January 9, 2018. The bill proposed to ban captive breeding programs and make it illegal to keep killer whales in captivity for entertainment purposes. "If return to the wild is not possible, the orca may be used for educational presentations, but may not be used for breeding, performance or educational purposes," the bill states.

How would any such legislation affect Lolita? Moskowitz defines educational presentations as a live display that provides "science-based education to the public" and includes "natural behaviors, enrichment, exercise activities and live narration and video content, a significant portion of which features orcas in the wild." Therein lies the rub. To date, the Miami Seaquarium has taken advantage of a gray area in defining the difference between education and entertainment, claiming that Lolita is an ambassador for her species and that she is educating the public.[75] As it was, the argument proved academic. Following strong lobbying by SeaWorld, the bill died in a legislative subcommittee. Despite the defeat, ALDF intend to work toward getting the law passed in 2019.

One thing is for sure. Lolita will never be forgotten. As a permanent reminder to residents of Miami and visitors alike, a 1,550-square-foot *Free Lolita* mural emerged in Wynwood, Miami, a place well known for street art, painted by Toronto-based husband-and-wife artists Shalak Attack and Bruno Smoky, a collaborative duo also known as Clandestinos. The boldly colorful mural with the haunting eye is located on the street side of the building located at 2247 Northwest First Place, which is owned by Philip Levine. "Miami should be known for its vibrant culture, not for the smallest orca prison in North America," said Levine. "This beautiful mural is helping make it clear that the Miami Seaquarium is no place for this far-ranging, majestic and endangered orca, who desperately needs her freedom."

In Washington State, there exists another mural of Lolita at Odyssey Middle School, Camas, created by dedicated seventh graders Taylor Redmond and Mia Parnell, who are concerned about Lolita.

For as long as she remains at the Miami Seaquarium, protests and demonstrations for Lolita's release will continue. In 2016 and 2017, two of these protests were centered in London and organized by the nonprofit organization Marine Connection to draw attention to where some of the funding for Lolita's incarceration was based.

Garrett and Berta continue their efforts to educate people about whales. Since opening in 2014, Langley Whale Center has moved twice to encompass expansion and runs a Kids for Orcas program. Junior advocate London Fletcher from Bellingham, Washington State, the youngest intern to

Above: Actor Adam Beach stands before the *Lolita* mural, Miami. *Howard Garrett*.

Right: *Lolita* mural painted by Taylor Redmond and Mia Parnell at Odyssey Middle School, Camas, Washington State. *Julia Smook*.

London protest. Counting up the years of Lolita's captivity. *Jo Phillips.*

work with Ingrid Visser, shows a maturity beyond her years helping younger children to learn about cetaceans and captivity.

Volume 3 of *Orcas in Our Midst: Residents and Transients—How Did That Happen?* was published in 2011 to explain the different eco-types in the Salish Sea and beyond. Garrett has also written an entry for "Animal Culture" for the *Encyclopedia of Animal Behavior* (Greenwood Publishing Group, 2005) and contributed a chapter about the rescue of Springer to *Between Species* by Brenda Peterson.

The popular Ways of Whales Workshop is held on Whidbey Island each year, featuring many excellent presenters. Welcome the Whales, an annual fun-filled family event based in Langley, welcomes the dozen or so gray whales that frequent Puget Sound in the spring. This small group of whales chooses to leave the main northbound migration and spend a couple of months around the Whidbey beaches, feeding on a secret stash of ghost shrimp known only to themselves. It is always humbling to see these gentle giants perfecting their high-risk feeding strategy so close to shore.

Orca Network's sightings network has expanded, with many more trained spotters on land reporting the presence of whales. These sightings are relayed to researchers working under permit to monitor the health and status of the Southern Resident orcas, totaling only seventy-four as of October 2018.

The dramatic decline in their numbers leads one to ask—what does the future hold for this critically endangered population? There is no doubt that this charismatic species is much revered. The iconic orca is the marine mammal of Washington State and symbolized in different ways. Where seaplanes were once used to spot whales as potential targets for capture, Kenmore Air, based in Seattle, has a striking black-and-white seaplane replicating an orca. The plane has been specifically designed to draw attention to the beleaguered Southern Resident orcas, honoring the annual Penn Cove commemoration by circling slowly overhead.

As proclaimed by the governor, June is Orca Awareness Month in Washington State, an example followed by Oregon and British Columbia. Orca license plates adorn many vehicles prefixed by the letters EW (endangered wildlife); Garrett and Berta have their own special plate, TOKILUV. Downtown Langley has a black-and-white police car with the silhouette of an orca painted on the side. This is not the first time a car has been used to draw attention to the whales, including Lolita. Publicity for her situation was raised by Swedish carmaker Saab in March 2007 when the

Langley Whale Center. *Author collection.*

Orca seaplane, Kenmore Air. *Richard Snowberger.*

company launched a thirty-second commercial titled "Why Constrain the Power of Nature?" The short advertisement featured a butterfly trying to escape from a room and an orca swimming underwater before breaking the surface into a breaching Lolita.

But time is running out for the Southern Residents. More than one whale has died recently due to malnutrition, with the summer of 2018 bringing a worldwide awareness of the tragic reality of more losses when, on July 24, J35 (Tahlequah) gave birth to a female calf that died half an hour later. Tahlequah refused to accept the loss, carrying the calf's body for seventeen days and over one thousand miles in a heartbreaking "tour of grief." Soon afterward, in September, J50 (Scarlet), a name given to her because of deep rake marks on her body believed to have been caused by other whales assisting the birth, gave up her fight for life. Although always small for her age (she was born in December 2014), Scarlet was described as a "spunky little whale" known for her spectacular breaches. Watching her become thinner and thinner and falling behind the rest of the pod was a graphic reminder of the whales' immediate needs.

Above: Orca police car, Langley, Whidbey Island. *Author collection.*

Right: TOKILUV car license plate. *Richard Snowberger.*

Where once they spent much of their time foraging and socializing, the "black and whites" are now conspicuous by their absence from the inland waters, their core habitat, during the summer months. Unless drastic action is taken to bring back the Southern Residents' traditional food of choice, Chinook salmon, the species is in real danger of extinction. One of the quickest options to address the food shortage is breaching the four dams on the Lower Snake River, namely Granite, Lower Monumental, Ice Harbor and Little Goose Dams, but to date, this controversial plan has lacked the political will to drive it forward.

Onyx (L87), Granny (J2) and Racer (L72) in Rosario Strait passing Mount Baker, Washington State. Orca identification Melisa Pinnow (CFWR). *Richard Snowberger.*

And what does the future hold for Lolita? No other orca has received such intense worldwide media coverage over a long period of time. More than twenty years ago, when Lolita cocked her head on one side and looked Berta in the eye, the activist made Lolita a promise—to bring her home. Where lawsuits and agencies have failed, now with the power and influence of the Lummi Nation, there is hope to see that promise fulfilled.

NOTES

Chapter 1

1. Visit Florida, member biography, www.visitflorida.org.
2. "Lolita Officially Named," *Miami (FL) News*, November 30, 1970.

Chapter 2

3. "It'll Be a Whale of a Wedding," *Miami (FL) News*, September 24, 1970.
4. "Strike Delays New Pool for Young Miami Whale," *Montreal (QC) Gazette*, May 23, 1970.
5. Untitled article by Norton Mockridge, *Schenectady (NY) Gazette*, July 3, 1971.
6. "Lolita Replaces Fat Hugo," *Beaver (PA) County Times*, July 26, 1971.
7. "Hugo the Killer," *Rome (GA) News-Tribune*, July 25, 1971.
8. "Killer Whale Retired," *Daytona Beach (FL) Morning Journal*, July 24, 1971.
9. "Hugo and Lolita Get Psychic Visit," *Boca Raton (FL) News*, October 26, 1972.
10. "The Killers Are Getting Cozy," *Miami (FL) News*, December 17, 1975.
11. "Killer Whales Accustomed to Man," *Lakeland (FL) Ledger*, May 10, 1976
12. "Sex Drive Stops Whale Show," *Palm Beach (FL) Post*, December 4, 1977.
13. "Not Even Death of Hugo Has Stilled the Waters," *Miami (FL) News*, March 29, 1980.
14. R.D. Ray, M.L. Carlson, M.A. Carlson, T.M. Carlson and J.D. Upson, *Behavioral and Respiratory Synchronization Quantified in a Pair of Captive Killer Whales in Behavioral Biology of Killer Whales*, edited by B.C. Kirkevold and J.S. Lockard (New York: Alan R. Liss Inc., 1986), 186–209.

15. "Feats from Flipper," *Miami (FL) News*, July 11, 1980.

16. "A Whale of a Charmer: Lolita's Become a Star," *Palm Beach (FL) Post*, July 24, 1981.

17. "Miami's Killer Whale Lolita Is a Happy, Well-Fed Widow," *Ocala (FL) Star Banner*, October 25, 1981.

18. "Killer Whale Cold to New Tankmate," *Sun-Sentinel (FL)*, December 15, 1989.

Chapter 3

19. "Livin' la Vida Orca," *Miami (FL) New Times*, July 8, 1999.

20. Orca Network, "Keiko's Story," www.orcanetwork.org/Main/index.php?categories_file=Keikos%20Story.

21. "Whale Watcher Biologist Ken Balcomb Hopes Liberating Lolita Will Unlock Mysteries of the Orcas," *Seattle (WA) Times*, October 23, 1994.

22. "Hurricane Andrew Update on Survival," *Orlando (FL) Sentinel*, November 25, 1992.

23. "Orca Battle Surfaces: Lolita's Plight Evolves into Whale of a Tale," *Orlando (FL) Sentinel*, March 19, 1995.

24. "Activists Want to Free Killer Whale Living Life of Riley," *Spartanburg (SC) Herald-Journal*, March 10, 1995.

Chapter 4

25. Jason Vest, "Lather Not," *Miami (FL) New Times*, October 5, 1995.

26. Dr. Gregory Bossart, letter to Betty Albertine, July 22, 1996. *Orca Network archives*.

27. "Seaquarium Revives Expansion Plan," *Miami (FL) Herald*, April 16, 1998.

28. Statement by Miami-Dade commissioner Jimmy Morales regarding Miami Seaquarium (undated).

Chapter 5

29. Hannah Sampson, "Seaquarium Trainers Will No Longer Perform in Water with Lolita," *Miami Herald*, June 1, 2015, www.miamiherald.com/news/business/article22831752.html#storylink=cpy.

Chapter 6

30. "Lolita's Miami Seaquarium Tank Doesn't Meet Federal Standards, Activists Argue," *Miami (FL) New Times*, March 11, 2016.

31. "Help Free Lolita the Killer Whale," *National Enquirer (NY)*, May 4, 1999.

Chapter 7

32. "Broken Pipe Spews Raw Sewage into Biscayne Bay," *St. Augustine (FL) Record*, March 17, 2001.

33. Petition to List the Southern Resident Killer Whale (*Orcinus orca*) as an Endangered Species Under the Endangered Species Act, www.biologicaldiversity.org/species/mammals/Puget_Sound_killer_whale/pdfs/petition.pdf.

34. Luke Rendell and Hal Whitehead, "Culture in Whales and Dolphins," *Behavioural and Brain Sciences* 24, no. 2 (April 2001): 309–24.

35. "Animal Rights Activists Mar Performances," *Miami (FL) Herald*, May 13, 2002.

36. Orca Network, Lolita Update #51, May 14, 2002, www.orcanetwork.org.

Chapter 8

37. "Inspectors Threatening to Close Seaquarium," *Miami (FL) Herald*, September 13, 2003.

38. W. Jon Wallace, CSP, MBA, to Russ Rector, October 12, 2003.

39. "Miami-Dade Officials Allow Seaquarium to Stay Open," *Florida Sun-Sentinel*, October 22, 2003.

40. "Keiko Makes It Clear His Free Willy Was Just a Role," *New York Times*, November 6, 2001.

41. Robert McClure, "Judge Rules for Orca Listing," *Seattle Post-Intelligencer*, December 17, 2003, www.seattlepi.com/local/article/Judge-rules-for-orca-listing-1132408.php.

42. NOAA, "Hurricanes in History," https://www.nhc.noaa.gov/outreach/history.

43. "Repaired Seaquarium Reopens Today," *Tampa Bay (FL) Times*, February 11, 2006.

44. *Federal Register* 70, no. 222 (November 2005), www.westcoast.fisheries.noaa.gov//publications/frn/2005/70fr69903.pdf.

45. "Seaquarium Open Again," Lolita Update #82, February 12, 2006 www.orcanetwork.org.

Chapter 9

46. U.S. Department of Labor, "US Labor Department's OSHA Cites SeaWorld of Florida Following Animal Trainer's Death," www.osha.gov/news/newsreleases/national/08232010-0.

47. "Gulf Oil Spill: 100 Days, 10 Lessons," *Miami (FL) Herald*, July 29, 2010.

Chapter 10

48. United States District Court for the Southern District of California, Case No. 3:11-cv-02476-JM-WMC.
49. NOAA, "Recovery Plan for Southern Resident Killer Whales," www.westcoast. fisheries.noaa.gov/publications/protected_species/marine_mammals/killer_ whales/esa_status/srkw-recov-plan.pdf
50. United States District Court for the Western District of Washington, Case No. C11-5955BHS.
51. ALDF, "The Loneliest Orca," https://aldf.org/wp-content/uploads/2018/06/ Animals-Advocate-Spring-2012.pdf.
52. U.S. District Court for the Northern District of California, Case No. 1:13-cv-20076-JAL.
53. ALDF, "Challenging the USDA for Licensing Miami Seaquarium," https:// aldf.org/case/challenging-the-usda-for-licensing-miami-seaquarium.
54. *Federal Register*, "Listing Endangered or Threatened Species: 90-Day Finding on a Petition to Include the Killer Whale Known as Lolita in the Endangered Species Act Listing of Southern Resident Killer Whales, Request for Information," April 29, 2013, https://www.federalregister.gov/documents/2013/04/29/2013-10024/ listing-endangered-or-threatened-species-90-day-finding-on-a-petition-to-include-the-killer-whale.
55. *Federal Register* 79, no. 17 (January 2014), www.westcoast.fisheries.noaa.gov/ publications/frn/2014/79fr4313.pdf.
56. David Kirby, "Could This Penalty Spell the End of Killer Whales Swimming with Trainers?" Takepart, http://www.takepart.com/article/2014/07/24/ miami-seaquarium--hit-with-fine-mishandling-killer-whales.
57. U.S. District Court, Southern District of Florida, Case 1:15-cv-22096.
58. "Lolita Activists Win Court Victory Allowing Protests at Seaquarium," *Miami (FL) New Times*, September 22, 2015.
59. GPO, "Listing Endangered or Threated Species: Amendment to the Endangered Species Act Listing of the Southern Resident Killer Whale Distinct Population Segment," https://www.gpo.gov/fdsys/granule/FR-2015-02-10/2015-02604.
60. U.S. District Court, Southern District of Florida, Case 1:15-cv-22692.

Chapter 11

61. U.S. District Court, Eastern District of North Carolina, Case 5:16-cv-00268.
62. "PETA, Animal Groups Sue USDA Over Seaquarium's Killer Whale Lolita," *Miami (FL) Herald*, May 18, 2016.

63. Dan Christensen, "Sexual Affair between Miami Judge, Witness Alleged amid Tainted U.S. Court Proceedings," Florida Bulldog, February 26, 2015, www.floridabulldog.org/2015/02/sexual-affair-between-miami-judge-witness-alleged-amid-tainted-u-s-court-proceedings.

64. Law360, People for the Ethical Treatment of Animals et al v. Miami Seaquarium, https://www.law360.com/cases/5783f192ef84bb05580001ad/articles.

65. Jonathan Kendall, "Feds May Change Their Opinion on Whether Lolita's Tank Is Compliant," *New Times Broward-Palm Beach*, October 3, 2017, https://www.browardpalmbeach.com/news/feds-may-change-their-opinion-on-whether-lolitas-tank-is-compliant-8099891.

66. "USDA's APHIS Refuses to Protect Captive Orca," Lolita Update #126, Orca Network, June 7, 2011.

67. U.S. Department of Agriculture, "APHIS: Animal Welfare Act—Marine Mammals (Cetaceans)," May 2017. https://www.usda.gov/oig/webdocs/33601-0001-31.pdf.

68. Michael Sainato and Chelsea Skojec, "Miami Seaquarium Leaves Marine Animals in Place During Hurricane Irma," September 11, 2017, observer.com/2017/09/miami-seaquarium-abandons-marine-animals-before-hurricane-irma.

69. "Two Dolphins Died at Miami Seaquarium after Hurricane Irma," *Miami (FL) New Times*, November 7, 2017.

70. Celia Ampel, "PETA, Miami Seaquarium Argue Lolita's Fate Before 11th Circuit," December 06, 2017, www.law.com/dailybusinessreview/sites/dailybusinessreview/2017/12/06/peta-miami-seaquarium-argue-lolitas-fate-before-11th-circuit.

71. U.S. Court of Appeal for the Eleventh Circuit Case No. 16-14814.

Chapter 12

72. Whale Sanctuary Project, "Whales and Dolphins: 'Who' They Are," January 1, 2018, whalesanctuaryproject.org/whales-and-dolphins-who-they-are.

73. Miami-Dade Legislative Item File No. 031783 Ref. 87, introduced June 11, 2003.

74. James Byers (RER), Chief, Regulatory and Economic Resources Zoning and Public Works Plan Review Division, email to author, February 21, 2017.

Epilogue

75. "Florida Bill Would Ban Orca Shows and Breeding," *Miami (FL) Herald*, January 10, 2018.

ABOUT THE AUTHOR

 Since the publication of *Puget Sound Whales for Sale: The Fight to End Orca Hunting,* author and certified marine naturalist Sandra Pollard has continued to advocate for the critically endangered Southern Resident orcas, including Tokitae (Lolita), the sole survivor of the capture era. Based on Whidbey Island, Washington State, she is a member of the Central Puget Sound Marine Mammal Stranding Network and a volunteer with the local education and whale sightings nonprofit organization Orca Network. Her writing career spans fiction and nonfiction publications in both the United States and the UK.